The Short-Term Rental Playbook

A Guide to Finding, Analyzing, Buying, and Managing Rental Properties with Risk and Diversification in Mind

Andy Wen

ISBN: 978-1-9994647-0-7 (ebook)

ISBN: 978-1-9994647-1-4 (paperback)

ISBN: 978-1-9994647-2-1 (audiobook)

ISBN: 978-1-9994647-3-8 (hardcover)

Special discounts are available for bulk purchases by corporations, associations, and others. For details, contact Andy@MoneyTalksWithAndy.com

https://MoneyTalksWithAndy.com

Contents

To all real estate investors, both present and future, great things await you.

Introduction

"**I**f it was that easy, everyone would be rich."

How many times have you heard that before? This statement is usually sprouted by people with zero knowledge about anything related to real estate investments. Some of these folk might even belong to the landlord-hating cult. Others might be well-meaning, but don't speak from experience. Misguided as some folks' opinions might be, I don't blame them. They probably have your best interests at heart and want to protect you from any potential harm.

Buying a property usually requires capital that runs in the tens of thousands of dollars, or more. This is a significant investment, and it's natural to have worries and doubts. Perhaps some of these thoughts have crossed your mind:

- Having spent a long time saving up for a down payment, is real estate really the best place to invest my hard-earned money?

- What if, after investing heavily in an investment property, I discover that I hate everything related to real estate investing?

- With no experience, I may unwittingly break landlord or tenant regulations and suffer the full wrath of the law.

- What happens if tenants or guests trash my place so badly, it ends up costing me more than I can afford?

If any of these reservations and fears resonate with you, let me assure you that you are not alone. Fear can be good, as it stops you from making hasty decisions that might put you in real danger. That being said, risk is one side of the coin and we must weigh up the rewards to see if an investment is worth it.

The other side of the coin are the potential rewards that await you should you choose to invest in real estate. Some of the things that you can accomplish include creating additional income streams, participating in capital growth of real estate, achieving financial freedom, retiring earlier than you planned, and pursuing your interests. There is no limit to how much you can accomplish. The more you invest in real estate, the greater the potential returns. You can invest in real estate to the levels with which you are comfortable.

Done safely and correctly, you can change your life, the lives of your loved ones, and open new opportunities you may never have had. I can't promise you all the riches in the world with zero effort or no risk to your capital. No one can. If you're looking for some get-rich-quick scheme, then this isn't the book for you.

Regardless of whether you plan on owning one, two, or more investment properties, it's important to set yourself up for long-term success. This means getting the right infrastructure in place and having plans for a wide variety of scenarios. I won't lie–there's a lot of work ahead of you, but it's worth it.

Let's dive in.

Do you know what "short-term rentals" *really* means?

Chapter 1: Short-Term Rentals–What is it?

"**S**he's a snake" my mother whispered holding my hand as we left our apartment.

Although a little boy I immediately understood that we should not trust that "snake" lady, or any stranger for that matter!

It was one of my earliest childhood memories. My parents and I rented a room in this big apartment block building.

The other tenants, like us, were never there for a long time. In fact, two weeks would be a long stay in that apartment building.

I didn't know it at the time, but this was my first experience of the short-term rental investment strategy–as a guest or short-term tenant. The short-term rental or rentals (STR or STRs) real estate investment strategy goes by many names. More names are invented every day that I probably don't know.

Before we get lost in a sea of what you think it means, allow me to summarize it in one sentence what the STR investment strategy really is:

Renting a property, or part of a property, for a "short-term."

What does "short-term" mean exactly? Is it one day? One week? One month? One year? One decade? The truth is, it depends. It depends on what the rules and law say when it comes to defining the period or duration of what constitutes "short-term." This varies according to location as different towns, cities, and countries all have different rules and laws.

For our purposes, "short-term" means a short-term rental agreement that spans, typically, one or a few days to maybe a few weeks. Let's say, generally, less than eight weeks or approximately two months. Short-term, to me, is not discussed in terms of months and definitely not in terms of years regarding the duration of the rental agreement. The legal definition of short-term depends on where you're based and there is usually less legal protection for individuals who rent on a short-term basis compared to those who rent for the long term.

Ultimately, you have a property, or part of a property, that you rent out on a short-term basis. You either own or have the legal right to let this place to potential customers who only want to rent for a few days or weeks. Tenants, in this case, are sometimes also referred to as lodgers or guests.

> **Note:** Exact terminology will vary depending on your location. It's like British vs American English; chips may not mean the same thing in the UK or in the USA. Just so you know, chips in the UK means potato or French fries whilst chips in the USA means crisps to the brits[1] – don't ask me why, this is simply how things are. This is similar for STR terminology such as guests, lodgers, tenants, and so on. It depends on where you are and what terminology applies. I'll use these terms interchangeably but make sure you're aware of the legal terminology for your specific location.

Now that we've defined what a STR is, here are some names that this real estate investment strategy goes by:

- AirBnB rentals

- Vacation rentals

- Holiday rentals

- Serviced accommodation

- House hacking

Naturally, this list is ever-growing and there are more marketing tactics to suck in potential investors to the attractiveness of the STRs' strategy. How else will people sell courses and services to investors if the strategy name (short-term rentals) sounds boring? If you can think of other names for this strategy, drop me an email (Andy@MoneyTalksWithAndy.com) and let me know.

Aside from all the fancy names assigned to this strategy, I'm sure you know more than you think you do. We've probably all experienced staying in a STR unit at some point in our lives...unless you've never been away and have lived in exactly the same home your entire life (which I think is highly unlikely). If you've never travelled or lived away from home for a short span of time, I'm both impressed and shocked.

Hopefully, you won't be surprised by some of these examples of STRs that most us will have some experience with:

- Hotels

- Bed and Breakfasts

- Guest Houses

- Staying at an extended family or a friend's place for a few nights

- Motels

These should be fairly self-explanatory. For example, if you've booked a vacation, you may have booked short-term accommodation, such as a hotel or bed and breakfast, as part of the holiday package through a tourism agency–or directly booking accommodation if you're one of those folks who likes to control every aspect of your vacation.

Another form of short-term accommodation that is well known is renting to lodgers and guests. Some call this "house hacking" but essentially you have a property that you rent out one or more rooms to individuals and there may be some shared-space arrangement where they have access to the kitchen, living room, and so on.

These are some forms that STR can take. You need to find an approach that you're comfortable with and where the risks and rewards are worth what it will cost you. We'll discuss the costs shortly, but let's get down to the crux of it. When it comes to STRs, you're probably thinking:

Is there enough profit or demand for me to enter the STR market?

Chapter 2: Demand & Profit: The Big Picture

For any product or service that a business wants to sell, the business needs to pay attention to both demand **and** profit. This is not an either-or requirement. A lack of demand in a product or service, no matter how great the profit potential, is pretty meaningless. The product and service you're providing is short-term accommodation and anything that you may wish to include, such as periodic cleaning, new sheets, towels, coffees, teas, and so on.

You can, of course, always find business and investment models that have minimal demand but produce massive profits for the few sales that do happen. An example of this might be selling high-end paintings or antiques by auctioneers—one sale can bring in millions of dollars in commissions. This may work for some business models, but not all.

With STRs, we need more than the proverbial one-sale-a-year gig. Depending on the location, you're looking at either year-long demand, where you can expect regular bookings throughout the year, or seasonal demand, where the bulk of your bookings will occur for certain seasons of the year.

In addition to having enough demand, sufficient profit is required for this to be a profitable venture.

Overall Demand for Short-Term Rentals

Looking at the STR industry as a whole, it's worth understanding the history of Airbnb to gain some insights into the sheer volume of demand and how this has changed the hotel & tourism industry[2]. Noticing that there was a shortage of hotel-type accommodation, the founders of Airbnb saw an opportunity to stay at different friends' properties for a few days at a time.

Sound familiar? Have you wanted to visit a location out of town and struggled to book a hotel at a reasonable price? I've experienced this more times than I care to remember, and it is very frustrating when there's nothing available for a suitable price.

In fact, STR demand has exploded so much that companies such as Airbnb and Booking.com have listed as publicly traded companies on the stock market. For example, Booking.com, owned by Booking Holdings Inc, trades under the ticker symbol BKNG and Airbnb Inc trades under the ticker symbol ABNB; both are listed on the NASDAQ exchange in the USA.

At a local or specific property-level, the only way to know for certain whether your particular STR is in demand is to put it on the market and see how it performs, along with the rates that you're able to charge, what the vacancy rate is like, and so on. You may also network with other STR owners and gauge what the demand is like from their perspective. Like any business, just because someone else is making good money does not mean anyone else is, or to what extent. Your results may be better or worse than other STR business owners; nothing is guaranteed.

Later on, we'll discuss some of the elements to consider such as where to buy, rental rates, and occupancy rates, as these feed into the subject of demand for a specific STR property. For now, have no doubt that there's definitely general demand for STRs that caters to a whole universe of people who only want to stay for a short time and have zero interest in staying for the long-term.

Now that we've got the demand side covered, let's turn our attention to whether there's any profit in running a STR.

Overview of Income, Profit, and Costs

Many moons ago, I had a six-month work rotation in Bristol, England where I stayed in a bed and breakfast at a rate of £49 per night. A standard long-term rental would have fetched around £500 per month.

You read that right. In about ten nights, the bed and breakfast brought in £490 which nearly matched the returns of a long-term rental and the remaining twenty days of the calendar was pure gravy. This was for one room only too, imagine if you had more than one STR unit available.

It's not unusual for a STR to make in a couple of weeks, or less, what a long-term rental would make in a whole month or more. In fact, some STRs can achieve much better returns compared to their long-term rental counterparts for the same property. Who wouldn't want to make this kind of profit? But as a savvy investor, you know there's no free lunch.

You're sniffing for the catch. Believe me, there's a catch. But first, let me confess—I've been sneaky and showed you the marketing trick that gets nearly everyone who is new to STR (or any other real estate marketing scheme). In fact, I did a couple of naughty things:

- Implied that profit is the same as income or revenue, which it is not

- Made it appear as if you can easily make ten times the income of a long-term rental in a short space of time

Now that you're wiser in spotting these marketing ploys, let's get into the profit equation, income, and costs of getting into the STR business.

The Profit Equation

Profit is revenue (or income) potential minus expenses (or costs). If you have more income than costs, you'll be in a net profit. If you spend more (expenses) than you make (income), you'll make a net loss. We'll use these terms interchangeably in the profit equation.

Assuming you've got a property that you're prepared to turn into a STR, you need to assess whether the income and costs of getting into the STR business is worthwhile of your efforts.

Let's tackle the first part of this equation, potential income. It's potential income, not actual income, until you get bookings and eventually get paid. This will inform you what the market is willing to pay for the STR space that you're offering.

Potential Income

The income part of the profit equation depends on many factors–location, presentation, seasonality, and what you offer as part of your STR accommodation. You won't know exactly what you can get until you actually invest in a STR, put it on the market, and see if guests book your place–this is where the market, aka paying guests, will decide whether your STR is to their liking and what they're willing to pay for it.

The quickest way to assess the income you might receive for a property that you're thinking about using as a STR is to analyze your closest competitors. Many refer to this as comparables, or comps for short, which is a common term in the real estate industry[3].

Whilst you're conducting your research, use this time to get familiar with the platforms that you're considering listing your STR on. Here's a high-level process to check out the competition:

- What are others offering in their STR for guests

- What furnishings, coffee makers, and other small details did you notice in the photos

- How is the presentation of their STR

- Do the listing photos appear professionally done or do you get the feeling that it's been taken by someone with no eye for presentation

- Do they have accessibility, smoking or non-smoking, house rules, pet, and other policies in place? If so, what are the main rules or policies

- What are the unique features that catch your eye

- *Lastly*–I mean it–*what is the rate* they're asking for

Notice how I put the income potential, or rate, last? This is because you need to be able to match, or beat, what your competition delivers to get that rate. Feel free to add your own criteria to the list above when analyzing your competition. The goal is to get bookings and paying guests for your STR.

Many people think getting into the STR business is easy—and it can be. Sadly, these are the same people who only provide a bed, bedsheets, toilet paper, access to a toilet, and expect to get the top rates that other STR businesses get. There's no free lunch here. Paying guests will pay what they think your STR is worth, and they'll be shopping around, comparing your STR with others.

We all want a good bargain, but what we love is a *great* bargain. Guests are no different. Will they rent your STR for $100 per night for the bare bones of a bed and bathroom that comes with toilet paper? Or will they prefer to rent a STR that offers everything you offer and also has a jacuzzi, an indoor heated swimming pool, an indoor gym, sauna, and more for $101 per night? Some might save on that $1 per night, but I'm guessing that ninety-nine percent of guests will pay the extra buck to get all those additional fun things in that upmarket STR.

We'll go into more detail later on, but you need to get your eyes looking for key things you want to emulate in order to give your STR a good chance of nabbing those high-quality guests that pay top-dollar and are more likely to respect your property.

Now that you've done some preliminary scouting on comps and what you might be able to command in potential income, let's take a look at the second half of the profit equation.

True Cost

Let's address the cost, aka expense, factor of the profit equation. Whilst it's fair to say that there are generally more costs associated with running a STR compared with a long-term rental, many underestimate the **true cost**.

The true cost can be categorized under four areas:

- Setting up

- Maintenance or on-going

- Time

- Emotional and mental health

No one seems to address that last point, but it's a cost you need to consider–probably the most important one.

The **set-up costs** might be minimal if you plan to rent out a single room in the home where you are currently living. If you've bought a property for the sole purpose of doing STRs, then you will need to work on the furnishing, presentation, and anything else that guests look for in the locale that you're in–i.e. you have to analyze the competition and either match or beat what they offer.

It goes without saying, but to make it crystal clear, any property you own–especially the ones you rent out–needs to conform with local, national, and any government regulations and legislations. For example, your location may have fire regulations that require clear exits, fire doors installed, emergency fire-kit readily available, and smoke or carbon monoxide and dioxide detectors installed in appropriate locations within your properties. Familiarize yourself with what the law requires of you and budget for this as part of your set-up costs.

The cost for setting up a STR will vary widely but this is often a one-off cost. Once you're set up, you should be good for a few months or years before needing to update or replace anything in the STR. This, of course, is subject to how guests treat your place. With increased turnover of guests, you're looking at increased wear and tear which you'll need to budget for. You may even have the odd guest that completely wrecks your place–again, budget and plan for it. This way you won't be as shocked when it actually happens. I hope you don't get terrible guests that trash your place, but better to be prepared than unprepared if you ask me.

Maintenance and ongoing costs have to be analyzed *before* you think about buying or starting any STR. If you're going to do all the maintenance yourself, make sure you know what the costs are for consumables and cleaning items. If you hire professional cleaning and management teams, you'll have to factor in this cost. Get clear on what you want to provide guests before their arrival, during their stay, and after they leave your place. You also need to consider other costs that need to be paid on an ongoing basis such as mortgage and insurance payments if you have these and consult qualified professionals where appropriate.

Your maintenance budget is linked to what you offer your guests. Cleaning or housekeeping and toiletries such as toilet paper should definitely be a staple. Will you provide coffee, condiments, little biscuits, snacks or beverages? If so, what type or brands of these items will you offer? The costs can vary greatly. As an example, will you provide instant coffee powder or a variety of Nespresso capsules, or both?

The time it takes to perform tasks is not something we see much of when it comes to real estate investing. Many misjudge the **time cost** involved with any business, especially the STR business. What you're more likely to hear from marketing ploys is how you can make lots of money and it's all "passive income." No one tells you how passive, or active, you need to be with your time commitment to have a successful business.

The actual time it takes to run your STR will depend on what services you outsource, if any. The most hands-off approach is a fully outsourced service where everything is run by a property management company that understands what you want and the platforms that you're using; this management service can handle almost everything from bookings to communication with guests, arranging for cleaning, housekeeping, and more.

The other end of the time cost spectrum is where you perform every task that is required to run a STR from booking a guest, check-in day, hosting period, and finally departure day. The time cost of these two polar opposites is something you have to weigh.

The final, and most important cost in my opinion, is the **emotional and mental health cost**. Do not underestimate the importance of your emotional and mental health. Whilst this doesn't factor into the profit equation directly, I think we can all relate to this in some way. There will be folks who are brave and don't place any importance on this factor–until they face a nightmare situation. Most guests are law-abiding, regular people, who will treat your STR with respect. There are, however, guests that will make you wish you had never got into the STR business. No one can guarantee you'll never meet these guests-from-hell, and there are some things you can do to reduce the chances of this happening. However, this does not guarantee you will never encounter nightmare guests. What you see on social and mainstream media doesn't help.

In fact, social and mainstream media can really skew the picture on the pros and cons of the STR business. On the one hand, there will be articles about how some folks are finding success and building an empire of STRs[4]. On the other hand, you'll hear about nightmare guests that trash a place leaving landlords to pick up the pieces–let's hope you're not one of the unlucky ones, or worse, that you get to the edge of declaring bankruptcy and losing everything.

A word of caution when reading any of these articles on social or the mainstream media: they haven't polled every single STR business, past, present, and future. This means that we have no idea whether the success or horror stories in the media are: a) the majority, b) the minority, or c) somewhere in between, of what STR businesses typically experience.

Truth is, you won't know until you take a chance and see whether the STR game will work for you. You may find great success, mild success, or no success and want to pull your hair out (assuming you're not bald to begin with before reading this book).

Increase Profit

Now that you understand the elements that make up the profit equation, you're better able to do some general research and hopefully come to a reasonable estimate whether your STR business has a chance of being profitable.

Whilst you're looking at whether you can turn a profit with the STR approach, this is a good time to think about how you can maximize profits as much as possible.

Since there are two parts to the profit equation: revenue and expense, you can:

- Increase income and keep costs the same

- Decrease costs and keep income the same

- Increase income and decrease costs

There's usually a trade-off in reducing costs and the time you commit to running your STR business. For example, you can do all the cleaning and housekeeping yourself, which saves on the cost of hiring a cleaning service, but this reduction in cost results in an increase in time you are required to put into the business.

Just a personal preference of mine, but I find it best to focus on one at a time and not pressure myself into optimizing every item in order to increase my profit. For example, focus on increasing income by adding more value to guests whilst keeping the costs the same; once you've increased your income a little, look at reducing costs somewhere such as bulk-buying toiletries and taking advantage of discounts or cash-back and other "frugal" techniques.

Whilst it's great to come up with ever more ways to increase your profit, keep one eye on the additional costs that need to be settled, such as taxes or replacing damaged furniture. Set aside some of your profits to cover these additional costs so you're not taken by surprise.

Increasing profit should be treated with joy as well as respect. What will you do with the additional profit? Will you reinvest this into more real estate? Or perhaps diversify and try other businesses or investments? Having more profit is a good problem to have. Beyond the emergency fund, which we'll get into detail later, be sure to have a plan for profits and excess cash, otherwise cash sitting in the bank will be eroded by that pesky thing called inflation.

Chapter 3: Return on Investment Comparison

H ave you ever heard someone say "all in" or "go all in" when it comes to some business or investment? It's a term or phrase that implies you should gamble everything you have on one bet. Personally, I really dislike this term as it reminds me of a gambling mindset and that is not what investing in or running a STR business is about.

Going all in might be fine if you're gambling a tiny amount of money, but it is not wise to do so in general—much less so if the sums involved are sizeable. The sums involved with STRs are sizeable and should not be treated lightly.

If you're determined to go "all in" with STRs, it's a good idea to pause and at least acknowledge that there are other opportunities out there. There's absolutely no doubt that STRs can be, and are, highly profitable for many, but there's no guarantee that you'll be one of these people.

It is, therefore, vital that you know there are other avenues that are profitable as well. I'm not talking about diversification; we'll get to that later. It's important that you *open your mind* to how a STR investment compares with other investments. The reasons here are two-fold: 1) understand how your investment compares with others, and 2) if this investment doesn't perform as you hope, know that you have other lucrative avenues to explore.

In the spirit of keeping an open mind, let's do a back-of-the-envelope calculation to see how STR returns compares against these other investments:

- Long-term rental

- Bank interest

- The stock market's S&P 500 index.

We will calculate for a full calendar year and some sweeping assumptions are made. For ease of calculation, let's assume you have a property that is fully furnished, and you own this piece of real estate outright. No mortgage or loan and no "fancy" accounting or creative financing methods. The property is valued at $100,000, which you bought with cash you had under your bed.

Let's say that as an Airbnb-style STR, this fictitious property can command a respectable $75 per night. The cost to have this STR fully managed by a property manager or management company is 35% of the gross rent. Due to scheduling between housekeeping and guest bookings, the average occupancy rate is at 50% for this STR.

The annual income for this STR is: $75 per night multiplied by 182 nights (50% occupancy rate in a year) multiplied by 65% (to account for property management fees).

STR income = $75 per night x 182 nights at 50% occupancy rate x 65% after management fees = $8,872 annually. As a percentage, this is $8,872 divided by $100,000 capital invested to give 8.87%.

As a long-term rental, this property would rent for $500 per month and is occupied for 11 out of 12 months of the year. This long-term rental will be fully managed and the cost of this is 15% of the gross rental income.

The annual income for this long-term rental is: $500 multiplied by 11 months (one month is vacant and unoccupied) multiplied by 85% (to account for management fees).

Long-term rental income = $500 per month x 11 months x 85% after management fees = $4,675 annually. As a percentage, this is $4,675 divided by $100,000 to give 4.68% (rounded up).

As with any real estate investment, there is the opportunity for capital appreciation (or depreciation) and the option to refinance and extract some equity which can be reinvested in real estate or invested elsewhere. For the purposes of this example, let's assume zero capital appreciation and no extraction of capital to keep things simple.

Let's not forget the stock market as an avenue to invest in. Investing in the stock market is popular with individuals as well as sovereign wealth and pension funds both of which are invested heavily in the stock markets globally. The average annual return, from 1957 to 2021, on the S&P 500 index was approximately ten-point-five percent[5]. For a $100,000 investment, the average annual return would be $100,000 x 10.5% which is $10,500 annually. Note that this is an average return annually, this can go up or down too.

The bank interest for the USA, Canada, the UK, and others in the west has been at historic lows since the great financial crisis recession of 2008. Prior to this, bank interest was in double-digit territory in the 1980s, decreased since the 1990s, and from 2008 has been at near-zero levels–feel free to check what each country's banking interest rate's history is like from a website that aggregates this information[6]. Let's assume that you get a 2.5% interest rate for your savings of $100,000; this would give you $100,000 x 2.5% = $2,500 annually in bank interest.

Let's summarize these figures below so that we can get a comparison of what you can do with a rough back-of-the-envelope calculation. With $100,000 invested, the annual figures for these four approaches are:

- Short-term rental: $8,872 or 8.87%

- Long-term rental: $4,675 or 4.68%

- Stock market's S&P500 index: $10,500 or 10.50%

- Bank interest: $2,500 or 2.50%

These figures represent a very rough estimate and are laden with assumptions. You should adjust these assumptions and calculations to perform your own analysis whilst being objective and keeping an open mind.

Feel free to revisit the STR assumptions above. Change the occupancy rate after you've done some due diligence for the areas you're analyzing. Adjust the nightly rate to one that you believe is more realistic. Perhaps you'll self-manage the STR and only need cleaning services, which you plan on including in your listing as a separate fee. Maybe you've got your own property management company and won't suffer the 35% full property management cost. These are all elements that you can adjust in the brief STR calculation we performed earlier. If you feel enthusiastic, take this one step further and see how changing these factors feeds in to the profit equation.

The purpose here is to demonstrate that whilst you're keen on STR, and it has great potential indeed, you must be objective and see whether your money can get a decent return elsewhere if you no longer wish to pursue the STR approach. Or worse, that you're forced to abandon the STR business for external reasons–we'll discuss some of these later.

We'll get into the real nitty gritty and perform a much more detailed STR calculation later where you can assess the potential profits for yourself. For now, know that even if you're unable to do the STR model, you can certainly pivot and make respectable returns on your investment elsewhere.

> **Note:** It's worth thinking about how easy it is to exit any investment. For example, bank interest and stocks on the stock market are (subject to any lock-in period) generally easier to cash and close out completely. Selling real estate usually has a longer process with more parties involved. The speed at which you can exit any investment is something to keep in mind.

Chapter 4: The Pieces

B ack when I started my real estate investing journey, I accidentally fell into the STR strategy by renting out a room within my property. This helped with expenses such as bills, mortgage payments, the occasional takeout dinner. *Note:* I still hold this property as of the date of this writing in late 2022.

Having been bitten by the real estate bug, I thought "how difficult can it be?" That was where my problems began. Thinking I was "all that" and failing to see that I needed the infrastructure to support my real estate investing journey. I'm not simply talking about a power team, but a few other things such as having a network, systems, backup plans, and more.

Much like Rome was not built by one person or in one day, your STR business will need the assistance of others over time. There is a time and place for each professional to step in such as legal support when you're looking at buying a property and cleaning services as part of check-out procedures. You don't need a lawyer to pop by for guests checking out, nor do you need cleaning professionals for purchasing a property–unless your lawyer doubles up as the cleaning crew!

Even with outstanding support and a great team, will everything go perfectly well from day one till the day you decide to exit? It's possible, but highly unlikely. What's more probable is that you'll encounter hurdles during your STR journey. Some hurdles will be easily resolved whilst others might take more effort or require a change in direction completely. It is, therefore, essential to have multiple backup plans just in case things don't go swimmingly well like we all fantasize about.

Let's kick off with the first piece that you need to have in place: making sure your ideas are legally allowed and ensuring your assets are protected.

Legal

Many assume that "legal" anything is to do with covering your **ass**ets. This is definitely true, but it doesn't stop there. When I say legal, I mean a lawyer or a team of lawyers or a law firm that represents you, the client, and has your best interests at heart.

To me, the legal aspect of my due diligence is to cover my blind spots, and all of us have many blind spots indeed.

Are you familiar with the entire, or at least the real estate portion, of your legal system? Are you familiar with the local laws, how it impacts you purchasing, and running a STR? This is an important practical point because if you don't understand the law, how do you know what you can or can't do, or the penalties for breaking the law?

This is why legal is an important part of the due diligence process.

For example, one of the common complaints I see every so often is where someone posts on social media something along the lines of "the evil local city bylaw officer, or homeowner's association, has given me legal notice that I cannot use my property as a STR, what can I do to change this?" Well, the short answer typically is "nothing you can do about it, move on." If they had hired a lawyer and done their due diligence *before* purchasing a property such as this, they would have likely uncovered that the homeowner's association can change their rules at any time and banning STR practices is completely within their legal rights.

We live in a more litigious time than ever before and it's quite possible to get into legal trouble with what you think might be an "innocent mistake." Do you know the law, and are you able to defend yourself, if you get sued?

You need to get a lawyer that has all these merits:

- Legally qualified in the specific area of law that you need support on

- Has specific experience dealing with the STR industry

- Charges reasonable rates according to their qualification, experience, and time constraints you're working to (if you want assistance immediately, this may come at a premium)

- Can represent you in the court of law if required

- Understands your specific needs

- Has a team of other qualified and experienced lawyers to lean on if they're unable to assist, call this the back-up plan in case one of their team is hit by a bus

Beyond the STR aspect of things, it's important to consider other legal aspects, such as inheritance or estate planning. You may not think you need it, but it doesn't hurt to think about it earlier rather than later. An incorrect set up can cause more harm than good and ultimately cost a lot to fix or reverse, if it's reversible at all.

> **Caution:** Not all lawyers are the same. There are different lawyers who specialize in different areas of the law. You probably don't need a lawyer who specializes in corporate or criminal law to support you with real estate boundary, tenant, or guest eviction disputes. A lawyer that specializes in real estate would be more appropriate.

Suffice to say that getting good legal advice is very much a worthwhile investment in its own right. Legal should be consulted for all the critical stages, from purchasing a STR all the way to selling your investment property.

Accounting

Your accountant might be your new best friend–provided, of course, your accountant has the right qualifications and experience in all things real estate and STR.

Similar to all things legal, you need an accountant or firm of accountants that understands real estate, STR, and your specific circumstances. No accountant worth their weight in gold is going to offer blanket advice on social media, and the ones that know their worth usually charge a decent penny for their advice. I cannot stress this enough. Get yourself a good accountant and have a meeting (or a few meetings) *before* you get your STR business or investment going.

First off, and in conjunction with legal considerations, you need to think about what kind of structure your business should be set up as. Corporate or company vs a personal business structure each have their pros and cons. This will bring up many things to consider, such as:

- Tax implications of company and personal business structures

- Allowable deductions, including depreciation

- Profit extraction and the most efficient methods specific to your circumstances

- Record keeping aka bookkeeping solutions

- Remote investor considerations

Let's take the record keeping point as an example of how easily things can go wrong. For example, your tax authorities might claim you made fifty thousand dollars of income for a year, but you claim you only made forty thousand dollars that year; the difference of ten thousand dollars could result in more taxes depending on your tax rate. At a fictitious thirty percent tax rate, this means an additional three thousand dollars of tax on the difference of ten thousand dollars of income. This doesn't even touch on the fact that the tax authorities might accuse you of fraud and other serious legal allegations, all because you didn't keep good records. As you can see, poor record keeping can prove to be a costly mistake.

The cost of getting your accounting process wrong far outweighs the cost of hiring a qualified and experienced professional accountant or team of accountants.

The last bullet point on being a remote investor (an investor who invests in real estate outside of their usual country or state) is something you may need to consider if you're investing in a different location than where you're based. For example, if you plan on traveling a lot, investing remotely, or staying in different countries or states, you'll need to consult specialists who understand cross-border accounting and tax law to advise on personal and company implications. Speaking from personal experience as someone who has cross-border tax considerations, I'd be lost if not for the support of my accountants in the countries where I need assistance.

Finally, you need to find a balance between the cost of doing things yourself and what it might cost to outsource some or all of the accounting and tax work. This ranges from bookkeeping, preparation of corporate and personal tax returns, along with the advice that you might need along the way, and much more. I often see people asking for recommendations for "the cheapest accountant" which is always a face-palm moment for me.

Hopefully, you have a better understanding of the importance of the accounting side of things and looking for a "cheap accountant" really should not be at the top of your mind. Instead, find an accountant that understands real estate investing, in particular the STR approach, and has a team who can support you in your endeavours.

Mortgage Broker

Mortgage brokers are only used to get the best interest rates on a mortgage, right?

Wrong!

As always, you have to look beyond the attention-grabbing idea that mortgage brokers are merely there to find the best mortgage interest rate.

It actually comes down to the type of mortgage that allows you to conduct a STR business and how it fits with your overall portfolio. The "terms" of the mortgage or loan are also critical. Terms here include the rules of the mortgage such as whether you're allowed to rent the property out or not.

Depending on the laws where you are, don't think that you can get a mortgage that is for residential purposes (where you live in this property) when your intention is actually to run a STR business or generally as a rental property. At best, this is a rookie mistake and at worst, this might be considered a serious offense like mortgage fraud that will get you in big trouble. Lenders have no patience and are very unforgiving when it comes to dishonest people.

Of course, we all want to get the best interest rate. But what is **more** important is that the mortgage terms work to your advantage. For example, one of the terms of the mortgage should allow your property to operate as a STR. In the event that you are unable to use your property as a STR, make sure you have contingency plans for alternative uses that are within the limits of your mortgage terms and conditions.

Insurance

If you're serious about getting into STRs, or any kind of real estate business or investment, make sure you tackle the insurance factor as part of your due diligence. I recommend you do this before you buy any real estate or get into the STR business so that you know the cost of insurance and you can factor this in to your profit calculation.

Perhaps you're of the opinion that insurance is a scam that insurance companies and brokers perpetuate to get you to part with your money. Maybe you firmly believe you can do this yourself by hoarding enough cash to pay for guest-related damage. It's possible, if you know ahead of time the potential damages that guests might cause to your property.

Surely guests trashing your place is the worst it can get? Think again. For example, if you have a swimming pool and host guests that use the pool incorrectly, serious injury or death might happen. You never want this to happen, but humans are unpredictable and there's an idiot in all of us—especially the ones that get drunk or do drugs and have misadventures in a pool.

It's highly unlikely that the average person can insure their own STR against every potential disaster. Consulting an insurance broker, or a few insurance brokers, will help determine what policies are relevant or compulsory, along with the associated costs. The insurance industry is complicated comprising of the insurance broker, underwriters, and more. I won't even pretend to understand the complexities of insurance policies or pricing. Suffice to say, an insurance broker will be able to break all this down and explain it far better than I could ever hope to do.

If your STR is listed with an online platform, it's worth checking the guest damages and insurance policies, if any, and what you are required to do to submit and make any claims. When it comes to guest damages, there's usually a limit to how much you can claim from a platform. Don't be surprised if some platforms make it difficult to claim guest damages; these platforms are there to connect guests with STR properties or hosts, they're not there to mediate who did what and when and how much the damages are. Sure, there's some mediation involved, but ultimately, it's your STR and if guests damage your property, it's you who needs to fix it regardless of whether you get reimbursed by a platform for some, all, or none of the damages.

Getting the right insurance in place is one area that you should consult an insurance broker or expert who knows what they're doing. If you get the wrong kind of insurance or don't follow the rules as stated in the policy that you sign up for, then you may not get paid on any insurance claims you make. Here's an extreme example: it wouldn't make sense to get car insurance to protect against guests damaging your property.

You'll need to do some due diligence to find the right sort of insurance policy that will suit **your** specific needs. Make sure you get an insurance broker that understands the STR business so that you get the required insurance protection on your STR. Any unique features, such as a swimming pool, might incur a higher insurance premium cost.

Double and triple check that the insurance policy, the terms and conditions, including the premium you need to pay, fit your requirements and the needs of your STR.

It goes without saying, but I'll say it anyway. In the event that you need to make a claim, make sure you have all the evidence required to back up your claims and follow the policies to a T to maximize your chances of getting reimbursed by insurance companies or the platforms where you're listing your STR.

Realtor

With the rise of the do-it-yourself approach (aka DIY style) and more "for sale by owner" type signs going up, should you use a realtor or real estate agent to buy, or sell, your properties? There are pros and cons to doing things yourself compared to leveraging the expertise of a professional realtor.

If you have the skill set and abilities to buy or sell your own real estate, by all means, more power to you and I wish you much success! Make sure you know what the laws are and what is allowed or not allowed when it comes to purchasing or selling a property.

For most people, though, it probably makes sense to use a trained professional to represent your interests. Naturally, you have to make sure you're working with a realtor who understands what you're looking for and can cater to your wishes. You're not someone looking for a residential property where you plan to live. You're not buying a piece of real estate for the occasional use once or twice a year or for a specific season of the year as a holiday getaway.

Realtors will always tell you why you need a realtor, and the DIY style folks will say you don't need to pay the unnecessary cost of a realtor when you can "easily" do it yourself. The reality is somewhere in between. These are some of the traits I look for when working with a realtor:

- Speaks real estate investor language and is familiar with STRs (bonus points if the realtor is also an investor so they know exactly where you're coming from)

- A great negotiator who can negotiate on your behalf and present your offers

- Has an ear to the ground and knows what the comps are, along with local knowledge and what is trending.

Use realtors to your advantage. Form a relationship with them so they understand what you're looking for. Whether you're looking for a fixer-upper or turnkey ready investment property that you plan to use as a STR, if they know your needs, then you can work with them to find a solution.

I've had good and bad experiences with various realtors in the past. Looking back, every single time I've had a poor experience, it was typically because either communication on both sides was poor or the realtor did not understand investor lingo and wasn't the right type of realtor for me. Make sure you don't make these mistakes; you'll save yourself a ton of time, emotional stress, and conflict with your realtor. Get yourself a realtor that understands the needs of real estate investors and you will have won half the battle.

Ultimately, realtors want their commission, and their goals should align with yours. Although sometimes a higher price is better for realtors (depending on their fee structure), the bottom line is that they would like to have some commission rather than no commission at all. They, therefore, want to have the transaction go through as much as you do.

Property Management

There are strong feelings, both for and against, property management or hiring a property manager. Before we get too emotionally charged about whether we should trust or use a property manager, ask yourself a couple of questions:

1. When you think of property management, do you get feelings of excitement or dread?

2. How do you feel about hiring a property manager to look after your property?

Depending on how you answer these questions, you may have a favorable or unfavorable opinion of property managers and property management in general. Some folks don't mind getting hands-on and believe that you can't trust anyone to manage your property better than yourself whilst others are adamant that the entire STR business process should be hands-off, passive, and outsourced to professionals who have more experience and knowledge in this field.

In some camps, there's some hostility to hiring property management of any kind and it's usually down to these three main points:

- They cost too much

- You can't trust them

- You can do a better job

These are all excellent points. The reason I bring up these questions and points is to bring both sides of the argument to the table so that we can have an unbiased discussion on property managers. Whether you're a fan of hiring out or think it's a terrible idea to trust a third party to manage your property, that's worth hundreds of thousands of dollars (or more), put your preferences and biases to one side for now.

If you're investing remotely, you're more likely to need a property manager of some kind. Whether this is on a full-time or as-needed basis, you'll need some boots on the ground to get things done on your behalf. If your property manager is unavailable, maybe they got rich gambling on some unheard-of cryptocurrency project and decided to quit the property management business at the very minute that you need them to do something, then you'll need to step in or arrange for someone else to step in at a moment's notice.

If you're renting out part of your own home, then it might be more convenient for you to get hands-on instead of hiring a property manager, which might be overkill. You'll need to have the contact details of suppliers of services so you can call upon them as and when you need to. The most common suppliers of services you want on speed-dial are:

- Plumber

- Electrician

- Cleaners

- Handyman or general contractor

You'll need to decide whether you can, or want, to self-manage your STR and surround yourself with the right service providers accordingly.

From a cost perspective, self-managing will be cheaper but requires more time on your part. As always, cost is only one aspect of the equation. The time and emotions required to self-manage your own properties should be considered carefully.

Taking a step back to look at the bigger picture as part of your real estate empire, how many properties do you plan on having and how many can you manage on your own? Depending on the size of your portfolio, you may eventually *need* to hire out some of the property management–a good problem to have.

No matter which way you decide to go on property management, have a plan in place and account for property management costs, whether you utilize it or not. This way, if you do use the property management budget, then you'll know exactly what profits you're likely to achieve and if you choose not to use the property management budget, your profits will be higher.

Network

This is the secret sauce section of my entire real estate journey so far. Networking. If there's *one* thing that you take from this entire book, this is it.

Unless your close friends or family have a history of working in some manner with real estate businesses or investments and therefore have a team of experts and service providers readily available, you will likely need to learn the ropes as you go along and create your own team. Fear not. You're in good company; I wasn't born with a silver spoon in my mouth and have had to work and network around the real estate industry too. I'm an introvert and not what many would describe as a people person, so if I can do it, I'm confident that you can do it too!

To give you an idea of how powerful networking can be in forming a team to support you, here are some examples of what I've found and the contacts that connected me to them:

- Good real estate investments through friends and tenants

- My lawyer through my property manager

- Trades people such as electricians, plumbers, and handymen through my network of friends, family, previous jobs, and real estate investment network

There's so much more that your network can provide. Don't have funding? There's bound to be an investor around who can fund your project. Don't have a property manager? There's bound to be a property manager or company that can cater to your requirements. Hopefully, you get the point–your network is a treasure trove.

Make sure you do your due diligence on anything or anyone you come across through your network. This means getting recommendations, checking reviews, making sure the people are "legit" and have the backing of other reputable investors or business people. Recommendations from fellow investors, especially seasoned investors, are usually best because seasoned investors tend to know what they're talking about. Always best to be cautious and vet things *before* you get into business with anyone to save yourself from future heartache.

When networking, be friendly, professional, and likeable; as much of a people person as you can be. This goes for any platform you're networking through; social media platforms, in-person meetings for real estate investors, or through introductions. If you're not naturally a people person, like me, then practice makes perfect. If you're an introvert like me, put yourself out there (a little bit at a time) and get some practice. There's much to be said about small talk and making people feel at ease. You do *not* want to come across as a person who takes, takes, and takes. Ideally, you want to offer something of value or interest.

Beliefs and religion aside, I want to touch lightly on this. Whilst I don't know how *karma* works exactly, whenever I've offered help–for free and with no expectations–I've been rewarded later down the line in some manner directly or indirectly. Whenever I've approached a meeting *wanting* something when I had nothing to offer upfront or in return, I've been disappointed. Don't ask me why things have worked out like this, but my best guess is that karma plays some part in the ways of the world.

All this to say that when you give freely and openly with no expectations whatsoever, you might be rewarded later on. Keep this in mind when you're networking, because people will remember how you made them feel and how you helped them, if at all. They will also remember if you were a "gimme, gimme, gimme" sort of person. Guess which one tends to be more successful?

Winners Create Systems

Think back to your most recent visit to a famous, well-known, restaurant chain[7].

It doesn't matter which restaurant chain you pick, just pick one.

Close your eyes. In your mind, walk through the exact steps that you think happen from placing your order at the till, all the way to receiving your order.

You may not know this, but chain restaurants have a procedure for every step of the process. From the point where you place your order to finally delivering the order to you. Every step is mapped out. This may seem too granular for many, but it's exactly these systems that have proven time and time again to work for these restaurant chains across the world. It's also why franchisees have to pay a lot of money to get into these franchises. This gives franchisees access to the brand, marketing, processes, supply chain management, and more. These are systems that have been put in place after a lot of trial and error over many years of implementation. These systems ultimately have a successful proven track record.

Make your life easier and put systems in place. Like these successful chain restaurants, you should aim to have a procedure for every step of the system, from booking guests, housekeeping, all the way to guests checking out and checking in the next guest.

For example, a basic three-step system for guests booking one or two nights might be something like this:

1. Book guest with payment confirmation

2. Greet and on-board guest on arrival

3. Guest check-out procedures

You can expand on each stage above to include every single procedure that you will go through. Stage one of booking a guest who has confirmed payment might include updating your STR availability on your calendar along with an introductory greeting, maybe a copy of the house rules, and so on.

If, God forbid, you are so booked up that you accidentally have a double-booking, you'll know that a procedure in stage one clearly did not work as this should not happen. You either get a booking confirmed and update your availability for that STR unit, or your STR unit remains available if the booking is not confirmed for whatever reason.

Had you *not* had these systems in place, you will end up spending a lot of time identifying the fault when you should be quickly identifying the fault and moving on to remedying and improving from that experience.

With systems in place, you can adapt and improve quickly. You'll be able to:

- Identify mistakes and errors

- Identify areas where you can improve on such as cost or time required

- Test things out, one at a time, to see if there's a positive or negative impact of the change

When starting out, be kind and give yourself some time to get the hang of things, but make sure you're developing a system on how to run your STR smoothly and learn from every guest booking. Only a fool thinks he (or she) knows it all. There's always something you can learn from and improve on.

Build a system for your STR and analyze what works, where can you improve, and which areas can you improve efficiency on in terms of cost and time.

Emergency Fund

The survival of any business is its ability to generate cash flow. Every business needs to have cash to pay for goods and services, and running your STR is no different.

Initial start-up costs aside, you have to pay for goods and services for guests once your STR is up and running. These include some of the following:

- Cleaning products or services

- Payment for loan or mortgage on your property

- Replenishing consumables

- Repairs or maintenance on short notice

These are simply a few examples. There are many more. In the event that you have no guests for a period of time, some of these *fixed costs* will still need to be paid, such as mortgage payments, internet, utilities, security services if any, and more.

Make sure you have a healthy emergency fund *before you begin* your STR journey so that you can weather any of the initial shocks that might come your way. Once your STR is up and running, it would be prudent to use some of the profits to bolster your emergency fund.

How much of an emergency fund should you set aside? It varies from person to person. Some investors like to put aside anything between two and ten percent (or more) of net profits from each guest. Others might calculate the potential maximum damage a guest might leave, along with all the fixed costs such as mortgage and insurance payments, and that will be the minimum emergency fund that will let them sleep well at night. For example, a potential worst-ever-guest scenario might leave me with the following bills to settle:

- Trashed my place completely, needs new furniture, coat of paint, flooring, fixing or replacement of appliances

- Regular monthly bills such as utilities, mortgage payment, and local taxes

- Additional cleaning fees due to the mess

Allowing for costs of a complete refurbishment would be wise. Never underestimate the ability of guests to destroy property. There might be some compensation that a platform might provide by way of insurance or claiming it from the offending guests, but this will take time whilst the place needs to be ready for the next guest.

You'll need to decide what a good emergency fund is for you, but my suggestion is to err on the side of caution and have a larger emergency fund than you think you need. No one complains about having too much of an emergency fund, but lots of people complain if their emergency fund doesn't go the distance.

Finally, it would be wise to factor in potential dry spells where there may be no or very few guest bookings for some time. For example, during the global pandemic of 2020, local and international travel came to a screeching halt. If your STR caters mostly to tourists, you would have taken the hit of having no guests, but your fixed costs continued, leaving you with a loss. We can't predict the future and having an emergency fund that can weather worst-case scenarios like this will leave you in good stead whilst the competition runs out of cash and may be forced to exit the business.

Platform Decoupling

Your business is to provide a nice, clean, and safe STR for guests. How do you get guests to your place? Typically–the vast majority in fact–list their place on platforms such as AirBNB, and this works extremely well for many.

Until it doesn't.

If you're getting guest bookings from a certain platform, these guests are not your customers; these guests are the platform's customers. In the unfortunate event that you can no longer list with a specific platform, whether by choice or otherwise, you need to have a backup plan. In fact, guests won't even notice that your listing is no longer there as your STR simply won't appear in the search results.

Here are some ideas you can explore to continue running your STR should you part ways with any platform where you list on:

- List on other platforms

- Set up your own website, advertise, and get direct bookings

- Incentivized word of mouth marketing such as offering discounts or commissions to guests who refer their friends and family

This isn't usually the place anyone likes to find themselves in, but life happens, and you may find yourself on the wrong side of a platform's grace. Plan for this possible outcome and know what your options are.

Plans for Exit

It's great to have some goals and to plan with the end in mind. By all means, set some goals that you want to achieve. The big problem with this approach is that it doesn't take into account that life happens. We all start off with lofty goals. Of course, we'd love to accomplish everything from starting a multi-trillion-dollar company from nothing, amassing a multi-million-dollar real estate portfolio, to curing cancer, ending world hunger, and more. Reality, however, is less glamorous. Life throws curveballs at us all the time and we must adjust our plans accordingly.

Although the focus here is to make a success of your STR investments, it's never a bad thing to have a backup plan that involves exiting the STR game in the future. No one said you had to stay in this business forever, till the end of time–which would be a really long time indeed. Here are a few examples of why people might want to move on from STRs:

- Made enough money and want to leave the business

- Getting old, done your time, and want to enjoy other things in life

- No longer interested in or this business wasn't what you thought it would be

- The profits are no longer worth the true cost

- Your STR is no longer viable as a business perhaps due to increased competition, reduced profits, or dwindling demand in the location, etc.

Once you've made a decision to exit a business, it boils down to two main choices: keep the property and change course or sell up and have a clean exit. The latter is self-explanatory and selling up for a clean exit, especially if your property has appreciated in value along with some built-up equity, can be a nice bonus to have.

Should you wish to keep that piece of real estate in your long-term real estate portfolio, a couple of possibilities comes to mind:

- Change your STR to a long-term rental, which usually proves more passive (less time and work required), and settle for a lower return

- Partner up with someone or a company that handles STR properties. This is similar to hiring a management company or manager for your STR, except you no longer deal with anything related to your STR. Instead, you'll deal with one person or company that provides a fixed or steady return whilst they run your STR under some sort of a sub-lease agreement (think rent-to-rent or rental arbitrage). Include processes so that you know things are running as they should be, and your STR isn't being used for "other" purposes that you did not agree to. See note below.

There are more ways to exit a business beyond the two examples above and I would encourage you to further explore ways you can exit the STR business. Whether you're thinking about an exit early or later in your journey, do what is in your best interest. No one will understand your situation better than you.

Note: if you end up partnering with or getting into some sort of a rent-to-rent or rental arbitrage deal where you're being offered "guaranteed" rent or income, make sure you go through the details with a fine-tooth comb and seek legal advice.

The typical way this works is that you sublet your place to a company, and this company rents it out for a higher rent than what they provide you in "guaranteed" rent. Everyone is happy when things work fine; tenants and guests pay on time, there are no vacancy periods, you get your income, the company gets their profit and manages your property as they see fit. The problem arises when there are no tenants or guests, lack of rental income, or some misuse of the property that you did not agree to–at which point, you're relying purely on whether this company is going to honor their word and continue paying you that "guaranteed" income and make right the situation. Another potential issue is when there are damages that start to eat or erode completely the profits that this company makes, who pays for damages to your property? As a savvy investor, you know there are no free lunches in life, and if something sounds too good to be true, it probably is. Seek legal counsel if you decide to go down this route.

Finally, it would be criminal of me if I didn't remind you to consult qualified professionals such as your accountant, financial advisor, and lawyer to make the right decisions for your circumstances, at that point in your life.

Chapter 5: Due Diligence or Get Ripped Off

I was at the drive-through of a famous global fast-food chain and looked at the pictures on the menu. After a few seconds of intense deliberation inside my head, I had narrowed the choices to either a couple of hash browns or a sandwich. Both were at the same price of $1.99.

I chose the couple of hash browns, paid the $1.99, got the brown bag of food, and drove home. Every step of that morning's breakfast had been planned, in my mind, on the drive home. The hash browns would go nicely with a cup of tea – Tetley tea with two sugars and one milk. I couldn't wait.

When I got home, I set the table and made my cup of tea. I opened the brown paper bag containing the hash browns. SHOCK HORROR. There was only ONE hash brown! I was so angry. My anger turned to the person who packed my order. Did they intentionally screw me out of one hash brown? Were they having a bad day and decided to withhold that one hash brown?

It didn't matter. I was home with my ONE hash brown and cup of tea. I felt really angry. After a few minutes, when my anger subsided a tiny bit, I managed to regain some composure, having been ape-shit mad about losing out on that one hash brown.

I replayed the entire process in my mind, from driving up to the order booth at the drive-through, placing my order, paying, and collecting my order. The picture on the drive-through menu quite clearly showed **two** hash browns for $1.99.

Although the world didn't end that morning, the rest of my day went downhill and was unproductive. I know, I know. It's only a buck ninety-nine and one hash brown. There's world hunger and other major problems and crying over one hash brown is insignificant.

The point is that had I done my due diligence and confirmed that I was getting two hash browns for $1.99 instead of one and checking the order upon receipt to confirm I did receive two hash browns instead of one, I might have been spared the pain of a crappy morning that affected the rest of the day.

Earlier, we touched on the fact that the STR industry has surged in demand, a big-picture view as it were. However, when it comes to specifics such as what location, which property specifically, what is the exact STR nightly and occupancy rates that you can realistically achieve; all these factors are extremely important.

My unfortunate incident of being denied the additional hash brown aside, let's say you buy a property on the basis that you believe it can achieve $1,000 per night as a STR. You go on to market it aggressively, on every platform, and it's the busiest season for that location. A week goes by, nothing. Another week goes by, crickets. Three weeks later, you still have no interest or enquiries from guests for your STR, much less any bookings. Puzzled by the lack of any interest by guests, you do some research and notice other STRs are listed at half the price of $500 per night and they're all offering wow-factor items to attract guests. No wonder your STR isn't getting any interest!

I cannot stress the importance of doing your due diligence to maximize your chances of buying a property in the right location that is in demand and will also be profitable. Estimating demand or STR rates poorly is like pushing an upside-down pyramid up Mount Everest. This doesn't even include the fact that some things beyond your control might further impact demand or profits, such as a global pandemic like the one in the year 2020.

Assuming that you don't want to run at a loss or misjudge the local demand, let's dive in to one of the most important aspects to nail down if you want to do well with STRs: getting your due diligence done right.

Chapter 6:
WWHRO–In That
Order & More

Deciding **where** to buy, **what** to buy, **how much** to pay, what potential **rental rates** you might get, and potential **occupancy rates** are all critical elements in STR and real estate investing. In a perfect world, you would buy an outstanding property in the perfect location, at below market value, command excellent rental rates, and have a one hundred percent occupancy rate all year round. Reality, however, is usually quite different. Getting most of these points checked off will increase your chances of success exponentially.

It can get quite overwhelming when faced with so many factors to consider but if you break it down into smaller, bite-sized parts–**W**here, **W**hat, **H**ow much, **R**ental rates, **O**ccupancy rates–then you immediately simplify the process and reduce the overwhelming feelings you may have felt.

This is a process that you'll go through several times before actually buying any property. It's not like buying a burger where you order, pay for it, eat it, and that's the end of the burger-eating process. The WWHRO process is more like tuning a piano; it takes repeated strikes of every single key with repeated comparisons to a frequency checker and other piano keys or chords to get it to the right frequency for that one key on the piano.

Note: If you're planning to use your own home as a STR then some of this may not apply to you, especially since your location is already fixed. Keep on reading this section because you might need it for when you come to invest in more STRs in the future!

Let's start with that first element–**where to buy**.

Where to Buy?

I wish there was a simple answer and could say "if it satisfies criteria A, B, and C, then this location is perfect–now and forever!" The truth is, real estate investing is location dependent for many things.

By this, I mean that depending on the location that you pick, you'll get the accompanying elements such as occupancy or vacancy rates (which we'll get to later on) and guest or tenant profiles that go with that location. For example, if you pick a location that is a holiday destination such as a ski resort, then the likelihood is that you'll have occupancy rates that are seasonal and the typical type of guests that you'll attract will be holiday goers, skiing enthusiasts, or skiing professionals. On the other hand, if you go for a busy city such as London, England, then you might be looking at higher occupancy rates and catering for various guest types ranging from holiday goers to locals (of the same country) looking for city getaways or people who travel for work.

If you have absolutely no idea where to begin, ask yourself some of these questions to get a better feel for what you, and potential guests, might look for in a location:

- Do you favor a seasonal, urban, or a bit of both type of STR?

- What kind of guests visit the locations you're looking at?

- Do you have a good understanding of the location?

- Are there local attractions that guests might be interested in visiting?

- What are the main transportation and accessibility methods available for this location?

- What local services (like garbage collection or hospital availability amongst others) are available in these locations–from both a guest and STR-owner perspective?

You should have a pretty good idea of what locations, and therefore the guest types, you want to target and the potential impact of seasonality on occupancy rates. In case you're wondering, yes, garbage collection is a thing, especially in more remote locations where garbage collection doesn't happen regularly.

As you can see, these granular issues need to be addressed upfront, before you sink significant amounts of effort and capital, in an STR venture. You don't want to simply go out and buy any piece of real estate and expect it to perform well as a STR.

> **Tip:** keep your guest avatar in mind as you go through this process. By avatar, I don't mean the movie[8]. I mean have a guest avatar as a fictional representation of your ideal guest in your mind so that you understand who you are targeting. From demographics, occupation, interests, and beyond, it helps to understand your ideal guest. Remember to be objective. Maybe try to imagine yourself as the guest. What would you expect from a location if you're on holiday or on a business trip? What amenities, local services, and transportation access would you like to see? If you're visiting a location for vacation, are there any main attractions that you definitely want to look up? How about if it were for a business trip that might last for a few weeks, what would you like to see from the location and STR that you might stay in?

Take this process one step further and think ahead. If you decide *not* to run a STR from your property for whatever reason, what are your options? Have a backup plan in case the STR plan doesn't go the way you expect.

Now that you've decided what kind of location you favor, you need to know **what** kind of property to buy and **how much** you can expect to pay.

What to Buy & How Much to Pay?

Don't ignore this section. In the past, I've ignored my own advice and didn't conduct the due diligence process discussed in this section and it usually ends up with me losing out by a lot. We're not talking a buck ninety-nine like the hash brown. I'm talking enough money to buy a new car (five- to six-figures) or at least a decent second-hand car (four to five figures).

Either way, who doesn't want to improve on their bottom line and increase profits? The best way to improve your bottom line is to pay below market value for any property. The next best thing is to buy at market value. What you want to avoid is paying above market value for a property.

In the previous section, you identified a general location such as a city, that you are considering. You now *need* a process to narrow down your search according to what your budget allows, what kind of property you can buy within your budget, what rental rates you're likely to command, and so on. This is where it gets a bit more granular.

The goal is to come to a realistic estimate of:

- What you can get for a certain budget

- What is currently on the market

Make sure you speak with a qualified professional such as a mortgage broker to understand what your budget is so that you're not wasting time looking at a million-dollar piece of real estate if your budget is closer to the half-a-million-dollar mark. Nothing wrong with checking out the million-dollar properties, especially if they're run as STRs, as it may give you some great ideas on what elements to include in your own STR, but be realistic if this type of property or budget is not within your grasp at this point in time.

Before you get excited and make arrangements for viewings with realtors and salespeople, do yourself a favor and get some preparation done. You need to have a good understanding of market values and comparables of real estate in the specific area where you're looking. Here are some reasons on why a little preparation goes a long way:

- Have an idea of what real estate is available the market right now such as number of bedrooms, bathrooms, kitchens, size of area beyond the walls

- Which properties are within your budget

- Know when price is beyond market value so you don't overpay

I always do my research before contacting realtors or viewing properties. Whilst realtors and salespeople have their finger on the pulse of the real estate market, there's no substitute for understanding the market firsthand. Although realtors and salespeople aren't evil or out to get you, they do have a financial interest in making sure you get a purchase (or sale) as they typically work on a commission basis, so they only get paid **if** you make a transaction. Nothing is said of the *right* kind of purchase–that responsibility lies with you in choosing a property that meets your requirements. It is, after all, your money that you'll be investing.

Here's my process of what I go through when looking at **what** to buy:

1. Navigate to a real estate search website that offers a properties-for-sale search function.

2. Zoom in or narrow down from city or general location to street-name level.

3. Add a budget filter and look at real estate within plus or minus one hundred thousand dollars of my budget to give a wider variety of real estate to review.

4. Browse every single listing and note details of what kind of properties appear from the search filters, such as number of bedrooms, number of bathrooms, and number of storeys.

5. Make notes on the listings that stand out and might be of interest to me.

6. Adjust my budget filter up a notch, so if the initial filter was a maximum of say one hundred thousand dollars, increase this to two hundred thousand dollars. Review the listings that come up from this search, beginning with the most expensive, and make notes of features that can enhance any property (at a lower budget) that I'm interested in.

That last point will very quickly show you how you can level-up your presentation to a higher standard and possibly command higher prices in the future. This short process, done over at least a couple of weeks, will give you a decent idea of **how much** a property is reasonably worth in the current market conditions.

Sometimes a market is super-hot and listings are there one minute and listed as sold the very next minute. That's great for the people selling, not so good for me as an investor looking for a reasonable price, or preferably a discounted market value price. One thing I've learned over the years is never to chase price. Chasing an upward price move means you'll likely overpay and get less for your money. You want the exact opposite of this. You can, of course, attempt to do a direct deal with the seller using more creative financial arrangements to arrive at win-win solutions, but that's a topic for another day.

Now that you have an idea of what's on the market, what it's likely worth, and how these fit with your budget and STR plans, it's time to dig deeper and look at the potential rental rates.

Rental Rates

Similar to the process of finding what to buy and how much to pay, you need to do a deep dive into the rental rates. I suggest you conduct at least a first pass at getting a feel for the rental rates that you might achieve before contacting realtors or property management companies or managers. Whenever I've asked a real estate agent or property manager how much a property of "X" bedrooms and "Y" bathrooms can rent out for, the figures that I've been quoted are typically higher than market rates. Perhaps they're all very optimistic people, or perhaps they figure that telling me a higher value is more likely to get them some business from me and they'll get the commission or management of that property. Either way, you need to have a good idea of the rental rates before investing in any property.

Unlike searching for what to buy and how much to pay, to find rental rates, we'll take a two-part approach. The first part will act as a potential backup plan should you need to go down the long-term rentals route. In the second part, we'll dive into STR platforms to uncover what the nightly rates you may be able to achieve in the area and property-type you're planning to deploy as an STR.

Part one – potentially using your property as a long-term rental if plans don't pan out as an STR. You haven't got started with STRs and we're talking backup plan? It's weird, I know, but starting with a backup plan in place is a good idea. It's like having a pre-nuptial contract in place between yourself and the STR approach that you're committing to so that if things go pear-shaped, you know that this is one potential exit strategy. Fortunately, you can change the terms of this prenup at any time and you definitely don't need to wait for the "till death do we part" bit to end this marriage with your STR property. In the event that you use this approach as an exit strategy, you'll know what your property might fetch on the long-term rental market ahead of time.

With that prenup attitude in mind, here's what you might want to do:

1. Navigate to a real estate website that offers a "properties for rent" search function.

2. According to the streets and location that you previously identified in line with your budget, browse the listings and note down the rental rates.

3. Make a note of the condition these rentals are in – are they top of the line move-in ready with all the furnishings and high-end appliances or are they mostly empty with no furnishings, dated décor that looks like they took styling tips from a seventy's fashion magazine?

4. Increase the rental budget and analyze the rental listings to see what higher-paying tenants expect and what higher-end real estate owners offer.

After this short exercise, you should have a reasonable handle on long-term rental rates if you need to go down the long-term rental route. Make sure you repeat this exercise closer to the time you want to get into long-term rentals to get the most up to date rental rates.

Part two of the rental rate process is hopping on a popular website like Airbnb (www.airbnb.com or platform of your choice where you plan to list your STR) and do a search for the location you're interested in and narrow it down using the filter and map functions.

Earlier, you identified the exact streets where there were properties for sale. Now drill down to those streets to see if there are other STR listings and check their nightly rental rates. The process is similar to finding a place you'd like to stay in if you were to visit the location of interest. The only difference is that this time, you're looking at it through the eyes of running an STR.

For seasonal type STRs such as winter cabins that cater specifically for winter holiday goers, you'll need to get an estimate of both off-season and busy-season rental rates. Estimating seasonal (or non-seasonal) data is a tricky thing and I default to slapping on a safety factor of twenty percent or more to give me a margin of safety, in case my estimates are off. For example, if the estimate of seasonal rent is one thousand dollars per week, I'll adjust that to eight hundred dollars per week and use eight hundred dollars as a more conservative estimate for my calculations. Anything above eight hundred dollars a week is a bonus. If I'm wrong, hopefully rental rates are not too far below my eight hundred a week estimate.

Non-seasonal or all-year-round STRs won't have to adjust for seasonal rates. There may be times when there's a spike in demand due to a popular event that people will travel to attend, think concerts, sporting events, and the like. For these one-off events, it's best to see where other STRs are setting their prices and make sure you price your STR accordingly.

The process of finding STR nightly (rental) rates might look something like this:

1. Navigate to the platforms where you plan to list your STR.

2. Search for the location that you identified earlier in **where to buy.**

3. With the map-function, navigate to the streets you identified during the **what to buy** process.

4. Analyze the listings that appear on each street and also nearby streets.

5. Make a note of your findings, the nightly rates, and anything of interest such as unique features and quality of the STR being offered.

Once you conduct part two of this process, you'll quickly see what sort of property (**what to buy**) and the associated **rental rates** that you can potentially command. Repeat this process for other platforms where you plan on listing your STR.

I would suggest that you have at least two platforms where you plan on listing your STR. This will give you a reduction of risk being associated with doing business on only one platform. Other platforms might include looking on www.vrbo.com and www.booking.com, which are two (currently) popular alternative websites.

Gentle reminder here: make sure you're looking at similar STR properties to what you want to buy. For example, if you're planning on buying a two-bedroom and two-bathroom property for STR purposes, get the nightly rates for properties similar to this and not nightly rates for hotel rooms or a property that has five-bedrooms with three-bathrooms.

In addition to conducting the rental rates research directly on these platforms, do a search on AirDNA (www.airdna.co)as well to get some more data points for your research. There's a lot of data available on the free version of AirDNA so take advantage of it. If you want to, you can unlock other features and data if you pay to access their subscription services. Definitely use the free version to begin with, for the cost of my favorite F-word, free, you can't go wrong. My only suggestion is that you don't treat the data as one hundred percent accurate but more as estimates that you can use as part of your due diligence[9]. Again, you may want to slap on a safety factor to be conservative with your estimates and calculations.

The only way to get accurate data in the real estate business is to buy a property, put it on the market, and see what rental rates you can get from paying customers. Supply and demand on the marketplace will determine what rental rates your property can achieve, which might vary with seasonality, economic times, and more.

> **Tip:** When you're conducting your research into this section, I've found it helpful to keep a map readily available such as Google Maps (www.google.com/maps) or similar. This helps keep me centred and focused at street-level and not be tempted to look at other nearby locations when I'm conducting my research into the rental rates and cost of real estate.

Occupancy or Vacancy Rates

We can't move on until we touch on the subject of occupancy or vacancy rate. In other words, you need to know how often your STR will be rented out or unoccupied. This is an important metric to be aware of and to factor into your STR management and calculations.

Occupancy and vacancy rates are, in fact, two sides of the same coin. The higher the occupancy rate, the lower the vacancy rate. For example, a ninety percent occupancy rate is the same as a ten percent vacancy rate. Get your brain accustomed to these terms.

Why do you need to know both terms? Well, you need to be fluent in occupancy rate and vacancy rate because different marketing tactics like to quote different data. Once you get your head around this, you won't have any fear of being tricked by smart marketing. We'll use both terms interchangeably to get you in the right frame of mind when dealing with vacancy and occupancy rates.

Unlike long-term rentals, there is a reasonable expectation that STRs will have increased vacancy rates due to the nature of the business. Busy metropolitan areas might have a lower vacancy rate compared to seasonal STRs, such as the winter or summer seasons. Either way, it wouldn't be unusual to expect some down time between guest bookings.

How do you find out what the vacancy rate is for the place and location that you're looking at? There are four main ways to get information on vacancy rates:

- Directly from an STR owner or speaking with people who run STRs in your network

- Obtain estimated data from a service such as AirDNA

- If you live in an area where you're confident there are a few STRs, do a bit of observing from a distance to see how often guests turnover

- Use the platform you plan on listing with as a guest to see, month to month, what dates are available or blocked (you can also make a note of pricing or nightly rates as you do this search as part of your due diligence)

With any of the above methods, make sure to account for seasonality and look at a whole year's worth of dates and not just a few days, weeks, or months. This is important so that you know, over a year, where seasonality kicks in, and how this affects your occupancy rates from week to week or month to month.

When getting data directly from a platform, make sure you're getting calendar availability for several properties or listings that are similar to the type of STR you plan on listing in the future. If you're planning on buying a two bedroom and one bathroom place, don't search platforms for STRs that have five bedrooms and two bathrooms in very different locations, say a remote area compared to the city center. Make sure you're comparing like with like to keep vacancy rates more realistic.

There is no substitute to real data that you collect yourself through running your STR, but this will only happen after you list your STR on platforms and start taking bookings from guests. Since it's likely that you'll be using estimated data of some form initially, it would be wise to include a safety factor to err on the side of caution in case the data you got wasn't as good as you expect. For example, if the data you collect suggests that out of twelve months (one year), your STR might be occupied seventy-five percent of the time, meaning your STR might be occupied for nine months out of twelve, why not decrease the occupancy rate from seventy-five percent down to say sixty-five percent? This will reduce your occupancy rate from nine months down to just under eight months (7.8 months to be exact) which is a more conservative number for your expectations and calculations.

The WWHRO Procedure

There's a lot to digest so far but I promise, this gets easier with practice. It's like riding a bike, the more you practice, the more proficient you become. I kid you not, this entire section is about building a strong BS detector so you know what's on the market, the rough value of what these properties are realistically worth, and also how fast or slow the market is moving. I've said it before, but I'm not one to chase an upward price move–I let others fight to pay higher and higher prices whilst I sit back and wait for fair or below market prices to return.

The where to buy, what to buy, how much to pay, rental rates, and occupancy rates–WWHRO–process is one that you need to repeat over a period of at least two to three weeks. You can expect to spend an hour or two on the first few days of your search and then anything from ten to fifteen minutes a day for the next two to three weeks doing searches and analyzing what's on the market.

The first few days may seem foreign to you, but by the fifth or sixth day, you'll notice the same properties around, the same average prices, the same sales prices, similar rental rates, and so on. Do this for another week and you'll have a pretty good understanding of the market. By the second and third week, there should be little doubt in your mind what the landscape of the market is.

Once you've got a good understanding of the market, you may *unleash* your enthusiasm and call some realtors and salespeople to get their comps and view properties. Given that you already have a good idea of the market, analyzing comps with realtors should be a walk in the park. If a seller runs, or has previously run, a property as an STR, then you've hit the jackpot in terms of data accuracy–do your best to get information such as nightly rates, insurance costs, seasonality, systems already in place, along with the usual "why are you selling" reasons. The additional information that you obtain from realtors and sellers will help you further fine tune the market value and rental rates before making any offers. See if you can come up with a solution (pricing, timing, and terms) that makes every party in this transaction happy.

> **Social media caution.** A seemingly popular way to get information, which I'm not personally a fan of, is going on social media and asking in groups, boards, or forums something along the lines of: "Thinking of buying real estate for STR in ABC location, what should I buy, how much should I pay, and what nightly rates can I get?" Besides the fact that anyone can make a comment, you have no way of confirming if what they say is accurate. The only way to check is to conduct your own research, which is the process I've laid out for you here. Going to social media isn't really the place to go for factual information of any kind. If you decide to do this, proceed cautiously and do your own due diligence.

To summarize the process:

1. Identify general location (where to buy)

2. Know what kind of property to buy at street-level (what to buy)

3. Analyze properties for sale to understand the current market (how much to pay)

4. Understand the rental rates for both long and short-term rentals (rental rates)

5. Know how often you can expect your place to be occupied (occupancy rates)

Take your time with this process and spread it out over two to three weeks. This isn't something you can or should rush. Getting a feel of the market takes time. If it's a super-hot market where prices are continuously rising and you're not willing to pay more than the market is asking, it might be a good time to take a step back, look at a different location, take a different real estate investing strategy, or look at a completely different investment altogether.

Make adjustments to this process to suit your style and requirements. We're like fingerprints and no two investors are exactly the same. If you're after a ten-bathroom and five-bedroom house, by all means hunt for these specifications, get the comps for this type of property, and run the calculations to see if this property works as an STR.

Jokes aside, this is a significant investment, and no one will understand your needs better than you. Do the research in an unbiased manner, come to a valuation that you're happy with, for both real estate prices as well as rental and occupancy rates, and go from there.

Chapter 7: Use the Correct Template

"This is completely wrong; you'll have to re-do the entire calculation," my manager grumbled in a huff.

He was not pleased; you could tell by the tone of his voice, holding back the anger combined with the fact that his face was turning beet-red before my eyes.

It was one of those long days in the midst of another busy tax season. This was back when I used to work in personal tax. The calculations my manager was referring to were foreign tax credit calculations. These are not straightforward to do, not to me anyway.

The company I worked for had processes and templates for almost every scenario, along with a rigorous review process to check, double check, and sometimes triple check tax calculations. If I got the calculations wrong the first time, someone would surely pick it up during the review process.

That's exactly what happened. The review process picked up the fact that, although I entered the correct figures, the template that I used was the wrong one. My manager probably spent some time reviewing my work before realizing that I had deployed the incorrect template. I can't say I blame him for getting a bit angry with my work, but I'm human, and I made mistakes.

This apparently minor issue would have easily caused our client to overpay, or underpay, on their taxes–neither of which is a particularly good outcome. Overpaying taxes usually means the client is unhappy, which is understandable, as not many people love paying more taxes than are due. Underpaying taxes, on the other hand, carries a risk that the client might get into trouble with the tax authorities in the future.

Suffice to say, I acknowledged the error of my ways, used the right template, and calculated the appropriate tax liability for the client. All was right in the world again.

Which brings me to the use of templates. I hate them, but I also love them.

In this day and age, it's so common to use templates that are readily available on the Internet or through paid courses. Proceed with caution if you do use these templates. These templates may work for someone in New York City (USA), but may not be applicable in London (UK), Gold Coast (Australia), or Banff (Canada). There may be *similarities*, but the legal, accounting, tax, and business rules are completely different for different locations and countries.

If you use the wrong template, you'll get really bad results like I did with the foreign tax credit calculation. Your accountant or tax consultant will happily charge you more to fix the errors in order to report the correct figures–this would be the best-case scenario. A not-so-nice scenario might be that you get audited by your government or tax authorities and they find you've been incorrectly doing all your record keeping and reporting, which results in more taxes, fines...or worse. Let's not dwell on this, because you're going to play by the rules, consult qualified professionals for advice, and get your processes set up correctly, right?

Using the correct template, though, will highlight the areas where you need to get additional information and simplify your life from both the accounting and business perspectives. You can update individual lines or entries easily and know exactly where you stand from an income, expenses, and profit or loss perspective–all at a glance.

With an abundance of caution on using the wrong template, I'm going to show you a "template of sorts" to detail income, expenses, and calculate the profit or loss for your STR. This will set you on the path to creating *your own* template.

Build-a-Template

If this is your first time creating a template to document income, expenses, and calculate your profit or loss, don't freak out. All we're looking to do is present the profit equation in a visually appealing format that gives you all the required information at a glance. Just a quick reminder that profit is the income or revenue your STR brings in minus the costs or expenses that you incur running it; this is the profit equation.

Whip out your favorite software, or pen and paper, and start creating your own customized template to record income, expenses, and calculate the net profit or loss. Don't let software stand in your way. Simply use what you're most comfortable with and take action. These days, I like to use Microsoft Excel as it has functions that allow me to add different columns, rows, or cells, once I populate my template with numbers. Before Microsoft Excel, I used Microsoft Word and a calculator to perform the calculations. Nowadays, you can use free tools that are built-in with your laptop or computer, or perhaps free online tools such as Google Sheets or Google Docs if you have a Gmail account. No matter what software you pick, just get started.

Your template can be as simple as three lines in your records:

- Total income for the year, $100,000

- Total expenses for the year, $50,000

- Net profit for the year, $50,000 (total income $100,000 minus total expenses $50,000)

This would be as basic a template as you can get. The point here is that you can make your template as detailed or concise as you wish.

My suggestion would be to list out items that come up regularly, followed by one-line that says "other" which allows you to describe what this extra one-off income or expense item is. Regular items might be income from guests and cleaning costs, whilst an example of a one-off expense might be replacing a fridge due to guest damage.

For a more detailed template, put together a list of every type of income and expense item that comes to mind and label these as either income or expense. If you'd like, feel free to include a brief description of each item. An example of an income item might be: income from guest number 105, two nights, rate of one hundred dollars per night, total income of two hundred dollars.

Input these two lists into the software of your choice such that you can clearly see the income in one section and expenses in another section. The difference between the total income and total expenses is your profit or loss.

Here are some examples of what might be included under the income section:

- Income per guest stay

- Nightly rate and number of days a guest booked or stayed

- Cleaning fees that you charge guests, if any

- Pet fees that you charge guests, if any

- Other fees (such as fees for additional guests) that you charge, if any

On the expenses front, here are a few examples to get your template started:

- Cleaning fees

- Replacement cost of items that need to be replaced often, such as perishables or towels

- Utilities cost such as electricity, gas, water, heating

- STR management fees if outsourcing the management of your STR

- Platform fees such as Airbnb and other platforms

- Other expenses, any one-off or random expenses that do not occur regularly

The income and expense list of examples above are supposed to get the gears in your brain turning so that you think about the income and expenses that you expect to see when running your STR. You should include income and expense items that you know you'll encounter. For example, you may have expenses such as insurance for your STR, maintenance costs, or mortgage or lease payments that occur regularly and you want to record these on your template. You may want to include a column for dates, weeks, months, or years, to keep track of this income and expenses.

It's impossible to have a complete list or know exactly what income and expenses you'll encounter during your STR journey. Therefore, you need to keep your template updated every so often.

Now that you've got your own custom template made, run it past your accountant so you understand the ins and outs of how your income, expenses, and profit or loss will be dealt with come tax or audit time. Get the all-clear before you start using your template for every STR calculation or estimation.

With your custom template set up, you give yourself an unfair advantage over those who are less-than-organized and most likely haven't consulted their team of qualified professionals at this point. The head start you have as a result of your customized template includes:

- Knowing whether your STR is profitable or not

- Easily identifying trends in income and expenses

- Assessing future STR deals using the custom template by simply inputting the numbers (after you've done your research, of course)

- Applying your preferred return on investment metric such as gross yield, net yield, cash on cash returns, and so on

- Knowing exactly how much was received or paid, when, and to or by which parties. This greatly simplifies the business and tax administration later on (make sure you keep the receipts and invoices; in case you're audited or required to show proof of income or expense in the future)

- Needing minimal updates to your template (only needs updating if and when there are changes to legislation, consult your team of professionals every so often).

As you can see, although it may take time to create your custom template, the benefits far outweigh the upfront investment to get this template in place.

Imagine if you had not gone through a vigorous process of setting up your template. When tax season comes, your accountant informs you that items you originally thought were allowable expenses are not actually allowed. This will decrease the expenses deducted which increases the profits your STR produced, and therefore increases the taxes you have to pay–which you probably did not account for because you didn't have a good template set up in the first place!

Suffice to say, it's in your interest to build a custom template that will serve you well for months and years to come.

Sample Template

Before going through a sample template and calculation, I want to repeat myself because it really is that important. **Be cautious of using ready-made templates**. Run through your custom template with a qualified and experienced professional so you know, without a shadow of a doubt, how your STR income, expenses, and profits or losses will be treated from the accounting, tax, administration, and business perspectives.

Let's go through what I personally include on the majority of my templates:

- Dates - either weekly or monthly

- Income - one entry per week or month

- Expenses - detailed list of each regular expense on a weekly or monthly basis

Setting up my template in Excel will look something like this (monthly version):

Monthly version

Month:	Jan	Feb	Mar	Apr	May	Jun	Jul	Aug	Sep	Oct	Nov	Dec	Total
Income													
Expenses													
Platform fees													
Cleaning													
Management													
Mortgage/Lease													
Utilities													
Maintenance													
Consumables													
Other													

Figure 1: Sample monthly template

That's a high-level view of what my template might look like. I list the income received on the top row that corresponds to the month that the income is generated. I could easily expand this template to a weekly format and change the top line to weeks one to fifty-two instead of January to December. The income line can be expanded to show guest details or invoice details, and the expenses section can be expanded according to any expense you have to pay, be it regular or one-offs.

Feel free to swipe my sample template, change it to make it your own, or use it alongside any accounting software you may be running. Be sure to get the approval of your accountant that your customized template is fit-for-purpose!

> **Note**: This template shows the accruals basis of accounting, not the cash basis of accounting– something to speak with your accountant about and how to account for income and expenses. Essentially, I account for income and expenses when it's due, rather than if and when I receive the money from a booking or pay for an expense. It's like buying things online with a credit card but paying for it a month later–the entries reflect when the transaction goes through, not when money changes hands.

You can get as granular with the details as you wish. The only criteria here is that the information is easy to understand and accessible, especially when it's time to do all the accounting and tax bits; the boring administrative stuff that gets overlooked is usually the one aspect that you should pay the most attention. Set up your systems and processes to log every income and expense item from the start and you'll have a much easier STR journey.

Regardless of what items you include on your custom template, make sure you know *exactly* what is happening with your STR on a weekly or monthly basis from a business perspective.

Sample Calculation

Let's assume you've done some research into an STR that has caught your eye, including details of the local area and services available to you (especially if you're a remote investor). You want to know whether you're likely to turn a profit, and if so, how much of a profit, on this investment property. For illustration purposes, let's go through a fictitious example and use my sample template to document the income and expenses.

Let's set the scene. This STR is located in a popular and bustling city that allows for STRs to be run and has several local attractions. There are many modes of transportation which include the bus, tram, subway, and taxis. The main local airport receives international flights every hour and is connected to all modes of transportation. Although there are hotels available, the STR sector in this area has significant demand. This location is popular with international and local tourists alike. Here are the income details for this STR scenario:

- Nightly rate of $100 per night

- Occupancy rate of 75% per month

For ease of calculations, let's go with an average of 30 days in a month. With an occupancy rate of 75% per month, you have just over 22 days of your STR being occupied or booked. We'll say you host 3 guests over the 22 days, meaning the average stay per guest is 7 days, rounded down to the nearest whole day. Cleaning, restocking, and any maintenance that needs to be carried out is done during the downtime between guests.

The monthly income would be 3 guests staying for an average of 7 nights multiplied by the nightly rate of $100. Each guest you host will bring in $700 of income. For 3 guests, the total monthly income is $2,100 (3 guests x 7 nights' stay x $100 per night).

On the expenses side of things, these are the details:

- Platform fees at 15% per booking

- Cleaning costs of $50 per guest

- Management company or manager to manage your STR at 30% gross income

- Mortgage or lease cost at $100 per month

- Utility bills for heat, water, electricity, internet, cable, at $150 per month

- Maintenance costs for snow ploughing, lawn mowing, pool maintenance and similar at $1,200 per year

- Consumables restocking at $50 per guest

First, make sure every expense item is represented as a monthly figure. For example, platform fees at 15% means nothing on its own and you'll need to represent this as a monthly figure. In this case, platform fees of 15% is applied either on a per guest of $700 basis, or on the monthly income of $2,100 for 3 guests. This results in a platform fee of $315 for 3 guests for the month.

This is what the monthly expenses look like:

- Platform fees, $315 per month ($2,100 monthly income x 15% platform fees x 3 guests)

- Cleaning costs, $150 ($50 cleaning fee per guest x 3 guests)

- STR management fees, $630 (30% fee x $2,100 gross monthly income)

- Mortgage or lease cost, $100

- Utility bills, $150

- Maintenance costs, $100 ($1,200 per year divided by 12 months)

- Replacing consumables, $150 ($50 per guest x 3 guests)

Once you have these monthly figures, plug them into your template and see what the totals are for the income and expenses. This is what it should look like if you have exactly the same income and expenses for a every month in a 12-month period:

Monthly Calculation

Month:	Jan	Feb	Mar	Apr	May	Jun	Jul	Aug	Sep	Oct	Nov	Dec	Total
Total Income (A):	2100	2100	2100	2100	2100	2100	2100	2100	2100	2100	2100	2100	25200
Expenses													
Platform fees	315	315	315	315	315	315	315	315	315	315	315	315	3780
Cleaning	150	150	150	150	150	150	150	150	150	150	150	150	1800
Management	630	630	630	630	630	630	630	630	630	630	630	630	7560
Mortgage/Lease	100	100	100	100	100	100	100	100	100	100	100	100	1200
Utilities	150	150	150	150	150	150	150	150	150	150	150	150	1800
Maintenance	100	100	100	100	100	100	100	100	100	100	100	100	1200
Consumables	150	150	150	150	150	150	150	150	150	150	150	150	1800
Total Expenses (B):	1595	1595	1595	1595	1595	1595	1595	1595	1595	1595	1595	1595	19140
Net Profit (A)-(B):	505	505	505	505	505	505	505	505	505	505	505	505	6060

Figure 2: Sample monthly calculation

Notice that I added a final line called "Net Profit" which is Total Income (A) minus Total Expenses (B) to easily identify what the net profit is for every month. Annually, the last column shows the totals for the whole year for total income, total expenses, and net profit or loss.

Based on this made-up STR example, where the figures remain the same for every single month (which is highly unlikely in reality), the net profit for the year is $6,060. As you can see, this "at-a-glance" view allows me to see what the net profit (or loss) is from month-to-month. If there are spikes in income or expenses, you can easily identify the culprit and drill down to investigate further.

Remember, this is simply a sample template with made-up figures. Use this as a starting point and create your own custom template.

Note: When evaluating whether a deal is worth further investigation, I tend to use a more high-level, generic template that has the big-ticket income and expense items to get a feel on whether there is enough profit. This high-level view will focus on the annual estimated figures for income, platform fees, management costs, cleaning, mortgage costs, and utilities to begin with; all the big-ticket items. Why focus on big-ticket items first? Well, my reasoning is that if you can't turn a profit on these big-ticket items, it's unlikely that profit will miraculously appear if you include *more* expenses as you dig deeper and uncover more information on a potential real estate deal.

If an STR deal looks promising *after* the initial high-level assessment, then I would be inclined to get more granular and flesh out expenses and income elements, drilling down to see if a more accurate picture can be painted on a month-to-month or even on a week-to-week basis.

Chapter 8: Buying a Short-Term Rental

H ave you ever seen someone selling ice cream on a cold, snowy, winter morning?

No?

Neither have I.

Dave is the ice cream truck vendor in question. Put yourself in Dave's shoes for a minute and imagine what he has to go through to start his business. He will have put in a lot of hard work to get his ice cream truck up and running. For example, he has researched the best street locations to sell ice cream, secured a loan to convert a van into a real ice-cream truck, purchased the supplies required such as refrigerators and power generators, obtained all licenses to run his business, and more!

All that effort and hard work means it takes a few months to launch Dave's ice cream truck business. Although the whole process started early in the year, let's say in April, by the time his business is ready to launch, it's November and the start of winter.

Can you imagine launching an ice cream truck business in the middle of winter? I don't imagine there are many people out buying ice cream. It's the wrong season for ice cream. Not many people will be in the mood for ice cream.

Feel free to disagree with me. You might be of the opinion that any temperature between minus fifty Celsius (minus fifty-eight Fahrenheit) to plus fifty Celsius (plus one hundred and twenty-two Fahrenheit) is good for ice cream. If you enjoy ice cream in all weathers and temperatures, you're in the minority because Google Trends shows that there's a seasonal trend and interest for ice cream; interest for ice cream is lowest between September to February whilst the period between March and August has the highest interest.

What does ice cream have to do with STRs? Not unlike Dave getting his ice cream truck business up and running, if you buy a fixer upper for the winter and ski season, do all the work, and get the timing wrong, your STR business will bleed money for months before seeing any income until the next winter season. You might be able to market your STR during the off-peak season as a cozy cottage, but you will have missed out on the season when the majority of your income is made. Seasonality may be less of an issue if you cater to guests who visit all year round, but even then, there's likely to be an increase in demand that coincides with events such as school holidays or annual conferences.

Buying an investment property is a big deal and you want to get it as right as possible from the start. So, what do you actually buy?

Ready to Go vs Fixer Upper

Next up for your consideration is whether you want to purchase a property that is *ready to go* or more of a *fixer upper*. Naturally, the one that is nearly ready as a regular long-term rental or STR is going to require much less work compared to one that might require fixing up or updating. Between these two main ways of getting into the real estate market, allow me to highlight three advantages, disadvantages, and the *common ground* between these methods.

Let's start with the common ground that is required regardless of which approach you take to enter the STR market. For any STR, you must have these basics:

- Good design, layout, and staging–hire professional help if you don't do this yourself

- Furnishing–from large items such as beds and dining tables all the way to bedsheets, towels, linen, kitchen cutlery, and so on

With inflation and rising cost of goods, it would be prudent to include a safety factor on top of the estimated costs for design and furnishing. I would suggest a minimum of ten percent as a safety factor; the higher the better, but use your judgement as to what you think will give you a good cushion in case you underestimate these costs. For example, if the cost is five thousand dollars, a ten percent safety factor would be five hundred dollars, and I would budget for at least five thousand and five hundred dollars for design and furnishing.

For cost-reduction on furnishing, use cash-back, store credit, and any other tools where you can to reduce costs as much as possible and get any perks that come along with it. You'd be surprised at how much you can save through two-for-one type deals, cash-back from using your credit card, store credit that reduces your purchase price, and more. If there are big sales days coming up soon, such as Black Friday, Cyber Monday, Christmas, or New Year's sales days, and so on, then it might be worth waiting for a few days before making your purchases.

In order to attract guests, you need to present your STR in the best possible light. Presentation, good interior design, furnishing, and staging is a must. Simply taking a few poor-quality pictures of a STR that is badly presented won't cut it. There's a lot of planning that goes into the presentation of your STR and we'll cover this in more detail later on.

If you choose to buy a property that is *ready to go*, there are advantages and disadvantages which you should know. The advantages are:

- Straightforward buying process

- Minimal work to get property up to STR standard

- Faster to get STR to market, and therefore faster to potentially profit from it

The disadvantages of this approach are:

- Costs more to buy the property compared to fixer uppers

- No opportunity to change the layout of the property itself

- Minimal equity can be extracted within a short space of time

Alternatively, buying a *fixer upper* comes with its share of advantages and disadvantages. The advantages are:

- Priced cheaper because there are issues

- Opportunity to revamp the place to your high STR standards

- Opportunity to refinance later on to pull out equity based on increased value

The disadvantages to fixer uppers are:

- Time and cost intensive for remedial actions

- Project management or shortage of labor and materials can hamper progress

- Takes more time to get this STR on the market, and therefore profiting from this will be delayed compared to the *ready to go* approach

Simply knowing these pros and cons gives you a lead over other investors who are clueless and haven't done any homework. You know the type I'm talking about; the ones that think they know it all after watching some series on TV, go out and buy the next piece of real estate they see, imagining that everything will go without a hitch, and think they'll roll in money the next week. Blessed are the ignorant...until they realize the mistake of their ways, then it becomes a nightmare for them to learn on the job!

With either the ready-to-go or fixer upper method, make sure you run the numbers for all scenarios and see what the costs are, total cost to buy, remodel or fix, and furnish. Run the numbers once, twice, thrice, as many times as you need and poke holes at it to see if you've covered all your bases.

Deciding on whether to buy a property that is ready to go vs a fixer upper isn't a decision you should rush into. If you get the timing wrong, and your STR location has a strong seasonality bias, ensure that you have plenty of emergency funds or a wide margin for error. Contractors taking a little longer or having difficulty or delays in getting material for your fixer upper can easily set you back a few weeks or even months. Do your best to avoid a situation like Dave's ice cream truck business, which was a complete flop.

Two Main Ways to Financing

Whilst you ponder which of two strategies is more your speed (ready to go or fixer upper), don't forget one key ingredient to all this–financing. There are many ways to fund a property deal, but the two main ones are:

- Cash

- Mortgage

Each of these property financing techniques have their pros and cons. This is where you have to lean on your network and team of experienced and qualified professionals for advice. Let's briefly discuss each one of these financing techniques.

Buy with cash. This is probably the most straight-forward financing method that is easily understood. You have cash that you inherited or saved up, and using this pot of cash, you purchase an investment property. You get full control of the property to do as you wish, within bylaws, city rules, and all that good governmental regulation stuff. Sadly, the return on investment isn't as juicy as other approaches. This is because your cash is deployed fully into one property compared to using a mortgage where you might only need to put up a percentage of the property value.

Buy with a mortgage. This approach is very popular with investors. The upside is that the capital required to buy an investment property is significantly reduced compared to buying outright with one hundred percent cash. Using a mortgage means that you will borrow money from a bank to fund part, or most, of the property purchase price. Automatically, this means an improvement in return on your investment. The down side is that you'll have to adhere to the rules of the mortgage contract, along with paying interest on the mortgage. The total cost of purchasing a property with a mortgage is higher than if you purchase outright with cash.

There is another approach worth mentioning as it's one of the marketing ploys that ensnares new investors with the promise of vast riches for zero risk, and that is the creative approach to financing or controlling real estate without having to put your own money in the deal. These are normally business transactions which are crafted between two or more parties that do *not* involve a bank. You are, therefore, free to create any arrangement when selling or purchasing properties, provided these are legally allowed in your region. If you plan on crafting unique approaches to purchasing (or selling) real estate, be sure to get support from highly competent and experienced lawyers who understand this area inside and out. Creative financial arrangements are not suitable for new investors and are best left to the more seasoned investor who understands the risks and rewards involved.

So, how do you plan on financing your property deal and how long will it take to get the financing in place?

Chapter 9: Timeless Process to Platforms & Guests

I was trapped in my own home. Not allowed to go out.

A week ago, I was walking in malls, going into restaurants to eat or pick up food, talking to people face-to-face, and maybe even petting the odd dog as I walked around my local area.

What caused such a dramatic shift in my lifestyle?

The global pandemic of 2020.

It hit me and many people around the world very hard. Going from being able to go out with no limitations whatsoever to wearing face masks, minimizing contact with anyone beyond my immediate circle, and a host of other restrictions forced me to alter the way I lived my life. My life changed within a matter of days.

Many of us had to adjust our lifestyle and businesses were not immune. Many companies changed the way they conducted business and adjusted their systems accordingly. Governments around the world introduced different mandates that businesses had to follow, such as when or how often you should sanitize your hands, how many people were allowed in different stores, and social distancing rules. These changes ranged far and wide and were continuously being updated. Businesses that had the option to deliver products to customers online reduced their physical store presence dramatically and increased their online presence accordingly; this was just one example of how businesses adapt to survive or even thrive.

Just like these businesses adapting to changes in the landscape, you, too, will need to adapt when the time comes. You need to be mentally prepared for this. In fact, not only should you be mentally prepared, you need to take action when change is required or risk being left behind.

Some things will remain the same whilst other things will need to change. Will people want to book STRs for work or leisure? You bet they will, but how bookings are made, what guests expect from hosts, design or staging styles, which platforms guests use to discover STRs, or pricing models of platforms are a few potential changes that might happen in the future.

Sadly, I don't have a magic crystal ball that tells the future, but savvy investors and business owners will acknowledge that changes are likely to happen and are prepared to change course and adapt with the times. Businesses that don't adapt usually end up being left behind.

One of the things that will remain the same is the general process to succeed with your STR on any platform. This short process will come in handy no matter what platform you're using to list your STR:

- Read and understand the terms, conditions, and community guidelines or policies of the platform–always do this FIRST

- Understand the platform and how it functions. Ask yourself a few basic questions such as "how do guests find a place to stay?" or "if I were a guest, what am I looking for?"

- Analyze competitors to see what they're doing and emulate the best practices

- Research and cater to guests' preferences

- Showcase what your ideal guest is looking for

- Optimize your listing by working on elements such as keywords (aka search engine optimization), photos, reviews, and copywriting

This process aims to master two things: (1) understanding the platform that you want to list your STR with, and (2) understanding guest or customer behaviour. Become a student of both the platform and guest behaviour and you will always see opportunities to improve.

The first part of this process is a no-brainer. You need to understand how the platform, or platforms, you choose to work with conduct their business. Part of this means going through all the terms, conditions, community policies, and guidance of these platforms. Do what you need to do to stay awake because reading terms and conditions isn't the most exciting of reads but is absolutely critical to conducting business on these platforms. You don't need to memorize the terms and conditions but knowing what the platform allows or does not allow you to do, how they deal with fees, guest damages, payment or refunds, reviews, cancellation policies, and so much more is critical to the survival of your STR business. Also, it pays to stay up-to-date with the terms and conditions so you can abide by platform rules and adjust course as needed.

Naturally, if you believe the terms and conditions are not going to work for you, then turn your attention to other platforms and avenues to attract guests to your STR. This doesn't have to be a permanent solution. Platforms can change their rules at any time and perhaps in the future the terms and conditions will be more to your liking, at which point you can revisit and see if you're prepared to conduct business on these platforms.

Rant: I often see people complaining on social media about how a platform has been unfair or unreasonable–which can and does happen. If a complaint is legitimate, contact the platform's customer service, be persistent, and cite their terms and conditions where relevant in order to resolve your issues. However, what usually happens is a host or landlord, let's call this host Derek, decides to list their STR on a platform and has an experience that is contrary to what he believes *should have* happened. He gives customer service a call, email, or direct online message and after a lot of to-and-froing, the platform's customer service sticks to their policies and Derek is left unhappy. Perhaps the complaint was about a refund that was issued to a guest even though he fulfilled his part as a host; who knows what the complaint was about–it doesn't matter. Derek's eyes are bloodshot, steam coming out of his ears. He is fuming at this point. So, what's the best course of action? Take to social media, of course, and launch into a tirade as to why they think the platform is so unfair and biased. You see lots of social media complaints by people in a similar position to Derek where they feel they got the raw end of a deal and that the platform they have listed their STR with is against them. Whilst it's definitely possible that platforms don't treat hosts as well as they do guests, it's more likely that neither Derek nor any of these people took the time to read any of the terms, conditions, or community policies and did not know what they were getting into. The platform dealt with the complaint in accordance with their policies.

The other part of this process is understanding how guests will find your listing on these platforms and ultimately part with their hard-earned money to book your place. It isn't good enough to list your place on a platform, present it poorly along with a poorly-written description of your space, and expect bookings to pour in. Whilst there is no such thing as a perfect listing, there are certainly steps you can take to improve your listing to appeal to guests. What appeals to guests will also change with the times and you'll need to keep up in order to stay competitive with what your STR has to offer.

Ask yourself: "what are guests looking for?" By answering this question, you can better cater to guests' demands, which will lead to more bookings. If you have no idea where to start and are completely clueless what guests are looking for, then you're in luck. There is usually a path to follow that will increase your chances of creating listings that will entice guests–follow those who came before you.

Chapter 10: Listing & Beyond for Success

In this chapter, we'll drill down to what you need to successfully run your STR. This will include crafting an excellent listing, things you need to have in place, as well as what you need to avoid in this business.

These days, people have a very short attention span, so your listing needs to grab the attention of potential guests within a few seconds. You also need to craft a great listing that speaks to your ideal guest and presents your STR in the best possible light. All these things will put the odds in your favor to (1) win the click when guests are browsing the sea of listings, and (2) win the booking with the information you provide on the listing itself.

Once you get those bookings coming in, you need to deliver an outstanding experience for guests. Maya Angelou famously said: "...*people will forget what you did, but people will never forget how you made them feel.*" You need to deliver the basics, of course, but if you can make your guests *feel* like they had an exceptional experience staying in your space, then you're on to a winning formula.

In the coming sections, we'll discuss best practices and things to avoid in order to be successful with your STR. We'll use the Airbnb platform as our reference point. Adjust your approach for other platforms, but the majority of what is discussed will carry over to other platforms.

Presentation Matters

Have you thought about how you are going to present your STR to the outside world? As an extreme example, do you have your coffee maker in the toilet, conflicting color schemes, or furniture and decorations in places they should not be? I hope not, and this is why you need to stage your STR appropriately.

Here are some options available to you when it comes to the presentation of your STR:

- Do it yourself or get friends or family who have a good eye for presentation

- Consult companies or experts that help with staging and presentation for STRs

- Observe how other STRs are presented (online or in-person) and emulate the best of these (make sure the outcome is well-coordinated)

- Browse stores, online or in-person, on how they present a space that attracts the kind of guests you're targeting

Once you've got your STR set up with the perfect presentation, listen to feedback from guests on what they like or dislike so you can tweak your presentation accordingly. This may mean moving things around and replacing or providing certain items that guests think should be there.

This part of the process is a creative one. Have fun with it, come up with different ideas, and see what designs and presentation work. I'm not a design expert, unfortunately, but will say that an overly cluttered or *busy* space is generally a turnoff for most guests and that's one design factor I would personally avoid.

A less cluttered space also makes for easy house-keeping and quicker turnaround times (cleaning, maintenance, re-stocking, and so on) so don't stage your place in a complicated manner. Think about it. If your space is like a thousand-piece puzzle, it will take more effort to re-stage and get it ready for the next guest compared to a space that is well-presented, but also laid out more like a fifteen-piece puzzle. *Simplicity* is part of the game here.

A word of caution: make sure what you present on your listing actually reflects what you're offering your guests. For example, if I go to a burger restaurant and they serve me bubble tea instead, I will be disappointed and possibly angry. It wouldn't matter if their bubble tea was the best in the world. I went in for burgers, not bubble tea. Likewise, if you do this with your STR where you project an image of one thing, but guests experience something completely different when they show up at your space, you will suffer the tsunami of negative reviews that will surely hit your listing and your STR journey will be short-lived. What is on the listing pictures must match up with the presentation of your STR.

Judged by First Impressions

First impressions matter. A lot. This means you need to showcase your STR in the best light to make an *outstanding first impression*. Whilst this applies to both your listing and when guests show up, you won't have guests showing up if you don't get the booking–and guests only book if they like what they see on the online listing initially.

You *must* be on your A-game when it comes to the pictures on your listing. If guests don't like the pictures you present on your listing, they won't look further. Imagine two nearly identical listings put side-by-side and the only difference is the pictures presented. One listing has bright colorful pictures presenting the main features of the STR in a positive manner, whilst the other shows dull and dimly lit pictures, mostly of the floor or walls. Which of these listings would catch your eye and which would you be more inclined to click on? I haven't come across any top listings that look like they were taken by a baby with a camera randomly snapping pictures. In fact, most good listings show professional-level photography skills and presentation.

Depending on your level of skill, time, and budget, you have a couple of options when it comes to obtaining great photographs for your STR:

- Do it yourself or get friends or family members to assist

- Hire a professional photographer or company

If you're doing the photography yourself, might I suggest that you take a look at the quality of pictures of your competitors before taking any pictures yourself. Once you know what level of quality you're aiming for, take one or two pictures and then do a comparison to see if you're at the level that matches or surpasses that of your competitors before taking more pictures. There are a lot of resources out there where you can learn to do this yourself, but this takes time and you may need additional gear such as lenses, lighting equipment, or photography editing software.

Should you choose to hire out, make sure you read the contract or agreement that you enter with the photographer or company. Get recommendations through your network as a starting point and check out the photography portfolio of any photographer or company that you plan on using. Also, make sure you understand who owns the rights and how the photos can or will be used (by you and the photographer) before you enter into any agreements. The last thing you want is to pay for a service and then not be able to fully utilize the pictures however you see fit because there are licensing restrictions on usage–which is why you need to read the contract.

Finally, don't forget that your competition has great quality photos on their listings–make sure your listing pictures stand out to increase the probability of winning that click from guests who are browsing listings.

Words Sell

As guests browse the online listings that come up, hopefully they're drawn to your listing because the pictures look great. It's unlikely that these guests will make a booking immediately after clicking on your listing. What is more likely is that these guests will skim read your listing first before deciding their next course of action.

Most platforms have a limit on how many words you can put in the description, so you need to be clear, concise, and paint your STR in an attractive light that will entice potential guests. If you're listing on multiple platforms using software, make sure you check that the listings come up the way you want, so your listing appears well-presented on all platforms.

There are generally five sections that you need to focus on when it comes to describing your listing:

- Title

- Description

- Amenities

- Information about the location

- House rules

The **title** is important to grab guests' attention. You'll want to include a good hook rather than a bland description in your title. For example, your title might be "two-bedroom one bathroom apartment", but you can spruce this up by using some copywriting (writing with marketing in mind) to "Stylish apartment next to Times Square." Putting your guest hat on, which listing are you more likely to click on? I know I would click on the latter because it suits my needs as I want to be next to Times Square and I wouldn't mind staying in a "stylish" apartment rather than just any apartment. If you insist on describing your apartment as a two-bedroom in the title, you can try something like "Stylish 2-bed apartment minutes from Times Square" which is still much better than the original "two-bedroom one bathroom apartment."

Next up is to **describe the space** that your guests can expect. Here are some things you want to include when describing your STR space:

- Summary of your space, why it's perfect for the guest you're targeting

- Unique features and selling points— point them out and how or why it is a great experience for guests

- What your space offers and what you provide as a host

- Areas that your guests have access to and which areas, if any, are off-limits

- Anticipate and address common questions like guest access areas (especially if you're sharing your home), number of beds and sleeping arrangements, check in & out policies, number of bathrooms, toilets, showers, and bedrooms, pet policy, smoking policy, and more

- Use paragraphs or sentences to structure your description and avoid the wall-of-text as this is not visually pleasing

- Use copy writing to paint a picture for guests on how they might enjoy your place

The description of your space is typically the longest section to lay out what experiences guests can expect with your STR. Use this space wisely to sell the experience that your guests might have if they book your space. If you feel you need some assistance with writing a good description, you can hire copywriters or companies that offer this service. Before you hire out, I highly encourage you to analyze what your competitors are doing, especially those with the special superhost status on platforms like Airbnb, so you can see how successful owners are writing their descriptions.

> **Note:** Don't copy another listing's description. Besides being in poor taste, you would be breaking copyright rules and it's highly doubtful that your place has exactly the same specifications as other STRs such as the same house rules, amenities, and so on.

When it comes to **amenities**, you should provide items that are considered *standard* for any STR. The easiest way to find out what amenities are common or expected is to look at three to five listings with great reviews. Pay special attention to listings that have superhost status on Airbnb or the equivalent on other platforms, if there is any. Within minutes, you'll quickly discover what your competition provides, and therefore what many guests will expect from your place in terms of amenities. Here are some amenities that many hosts offer, which can be considered *standard* in many locations:

- WiFi

- Coffee maker

- Microwave

- Kitchen utensils

- Refrigerator

- Smoke alarm

- Heating and air conditioning

- TV

- Iron

- Hair dryer

- Hot water

- Additional towels, bedsheets, blankets, etc.

- Toilet paper, shampoo, toiletries

There are many more amenities you could add, but these are the common ones that I've come across. To be clear, you don't *have* to provide these common items, but if your competitors provide them and you don't, then you're short-changing yourself and giving your competition the upper hand–especially if it is easily within your means to provide basic items but you choose not to.

Providing information about your **location** and local neighbourhood goes a long way with helping guests decide on your place.. Be sure to point out the main attractions, any events or restaurants that guests may wish to visit or enjoy. Including information about travel or local transportation systems is a good idea as you never know where guests are traveling from.

Finally, put together a list of your **house rules** that guests are expected to abide by. We live in a society that has clear boundaries and laws that govern what we can or cannot do. Likewise, your guests should be under no illusion as to what those boundaries are for your place, as set out via the house rules. You may have alluded to some of these rules earlier in your description, such as whether you have a pet or smoking policy in place, but the house rules are where you make it crystal clear on what is allowed, allowed with conditions, or downright not tolerated. Every host is going to have a different set of rules, but here's a list of some policies to consider and be clear on where you stand:

- Check in and check out policy and if there is any flexibility on this

- Maximum number of guests, visitors, and any additional fees

- Pets, no pets, pets with supervision, or support animal policy

- Smoking or no smoking policy and if there are designated smoking areas

- Whether parties or events are allowed

- Third-party bookings, cancellation and refunds policy (as set out and abiding by platform rules) if there are any

- Child or baby policy and if your place is child or baby friendly

- Noise policy

Feel free to add your own policies and set your house rules accordingly. The only caveat is that you need to make sure that all your house rules are in alignment with the laws in your location and are within the listing platform's rules. For example, if your location does not allow you to say no pets then please, don't say no pets because this will be in clear violation of your local laws. What is legal in one location may not be legal in another region or country. If in doubt, consult with your team of qualified professionals for guidance.

A word on keywords and search engine optimization: generally, you want to write everything in your listing that is made-for-humans-to-read and not made-for-computers-to-index. I occasionally come across listings that have been poorly written with zero copywriting or any effort to entice guests to their STR but has lots of targeted phrases, or keywords, that look like they got it straight from a search engine. The search engine that guests use to find a place is not the same search engine that we use for searching for information online, and it's ultimately the guest that books your place and not an online search engine. I would encourage you to focus on writing a listing with your target guest in mind and if the opportunity presents itself, sprinkle in some keywords—provided it flows naturally, of course.

Getting and Dealing with Reviews

It's no secret that reviews are important–for any platform–from both a guest and host perspective. Before customers buy any product or service, they look at reviews which helps shape their buying decision. If you're looking to book accommodation for your holiday, you, too, will look at reviews before you make that booking.

For example, on Airbnb, potential guests might look at reviews to see if a listing is good or not so good, which reflects how the host conducts their business. Likewise, hosts look at guest reviews to see how well-behaved guests were in the past. The point is reviews are important and guests and hosts alike will read reviews before deciding whether a place is a good fit for both parties.

If you're starting from ground zero, you won't have any reviews. So, how do you go about getting some? Well, after a guest completes their stay in your STR, they will automatically be contacted by the platform with a request for feedback and review. You can also include a review request as part of your check-out process or in a guest book if you have one–these are a couple of options that you can consider when asking for guests to leave a review of their stay at your place.

Whilst we all hope to get great five-star reviews, sometimes guest feedback may sting if it doesn't align with your expectations. If you receive less-than-positive stars or reviews, use this as a learning tool to improve your service and STR business according to the feedback guests offer you. Reflect on these reviews and adjust course accordingly to improve the experience for the next guest.

On the other hand, some guests have poor behaviour and may resort to black-mail-like, or retaliatory, tactics through negative or one-star reviews. An example that comes to mind is for a guest to request for a refund during their stay and say that if they don't get a refund, you'll get a bad review. In these instances, make sure you document everything and get in touch with the platform if you believe it is against the platform's review policies. You should have read the platform terms and conditions before you listed your STR so you should be well-versed in how retaliatory reviews will be handled. If you haven't read the platform terms and conditions, now is the perfect time for you to go read it.

In turn, you may be asked to review guests and their stay at your STR. Be factual, professional and avoid anything that cannot be evidenced. How you feel is irrelevant to whether a guest followed your house rules or not. Imagine a guest decides to break all your house rules and damage your property—yes, some guests really go out of their way to be bad—instead of talking about how you felt, stick with the facts and state that the guest did not follow your house rules, damaged property, and that you would not host them again or that they are more suitable for hotel accommodation. Stick with the facts and platform policies is your best course of action when it comes to providing guest-reviews.

> **Note:** If there are reviews that are clearly against the platform's policies, but the platform refuses to remove it upon your initial request, don't give up. Contact the platforms customer service again with a clear explanation of what policies are being broken and why the reviews should be removed. You may need to be persistent, but it's in the platform's best interest to adhere to their own policies.

Besides learning from less-than-great reviews, if you deliver a fantastic guest experience, have open lines of communication, fix anything that needs fixing immediately, you are likely to see positive reviews over time.

The Key to Good Communication

Having lived on three continents and done some traveling, I can tell you that leaving the comforts of my home, a safe space, to travel to another location, will always stress me out and give me anxiety. One of the many concerns is how will I reach my accommodation and will everything go smoothly.

Wouldn't it be nice if someone was there to assure me that, accommodation wise, everything is set up and ready for my arrival? This would go a long way in reducing my stress and certainly help settle my nerves—at least I wouldn't have to worry about anything accommodation related.

This is where you can really shine—by communicating with your guest to enhance their experience. Put yourself in your guest's shoes for the whole process, from sitting at home, browsing online listings on platforms like Airbnb, stumbling across your listing, clicking through to read the details about your place, making the booking, traveling, checking in, staying and sight-seeing for the duration of the booking, checking out, and traveling back to their home. You know practically every step of this entire process and are in a great position to help your guest from start to finish.

By communicating effectively with your guests, you can give them a sense of safety and security that you are there for them as an attentive, caring, and helpful host and everything will go smoothly–at least as far as the accommodation goes.

Don't worry if you're not a great communicator. Communication is an art, but there are some things that you can use right off the bat to give yourself a flying start. Here are three things you need to do for all guest communications:

- Be professional and courteous–this creates a good experience and don't forget that the platform can see the messages between you and your guests via their messaging system

- Be open and honest–set expectations from the start so guests know what your place offers and what they can expect

- Respond promptly to guest messages

These are the bare essentials that you must have when communicating with your guests. It's easier than it looks and, with time, you'll develop your own voice. Use each message and guest experience to improve your communication skills and you'll do fine.

There are six critical moments when you must communicate with your guests. Failure to do so doesn't mean the end of the world, fortunately, but it does mean a missed opportunity to impress your guests with your attentiveness and appearing like you're doing everything you can to make their stay a memorable one. It also means that you might get repeat questions that you might otherwise cover with your pro-active messages. Here are the critical points at which you should communicate with your guests, along with a brief explanation of each point:

1. **Shortly after a guest makes a booking:** If you haven't heard from the guest, don't be shy to drop your guest that first message. A "welcome" or "thank you for booking" note, confirmation of their booking details, some information about the local area, ask one or two questions such as the purpose of their visit (if you haven't previously communicated with the guest earlier on–some guests message hosts before making a booking) or who will accompany them so you can tailor your messages

to your guest's circumstances, providing your guest with a list of items that they can expect from you closer to their arrival (such as detailed directions to your place or specific check-in and check-out instructions), are a few ideas on what you may want to include in your welcome message. This might be your first contact with the guest, so make sure you're professional, courteous, and that this is how you would like to be welcomed if you were a guest.

2. **A few days before they arrive:** At this stage, your guest might have some anxiety over their trip such as having some reservations about the travel or accommodation. Providing your guest with clear and concise details of a few things will greatly reduce their stress levels. Information on specific directions to get to your place, the exact check-in process, how they will access your place, and a friendly note to say you look forward to hosting them soon can sooth your guest's anxieties.

3. **Go times:** This time-critical zone spans a few hours before and after check-in. This is where your guest is experiencing high excitement or anxiety levels. Guess what your job is? You guessed it, to make this process as seamless and pain-free as humanly possible for your guest. A few hours before check-in, send your guest a message with key details similar to what you did in point two. Specific directions to your place, check-in procedures such as how to gain access to your place (whether you're welcoming them in-person or remotely via a lockbox system where you furnish them with the code to access said lockbox or some other alternative). If you previously provided this information, provide it again! You will be surprised at how many guests want this information handy without having the hassle of looking through all their previous messages. Make this information easy to read and understand, anything to reduce the thinking required by your already-stressed-out guest. Upon check-in up to a few hours after the guest arrives, reach out to them to see that they arrived safe and sound and ask if they have everything they need for their stay. If you offer a welcome hamper or gift, mention this in your message, along with a brief explanation of what is included in the welcome package. Gently remind of your house rules or request that they read the house-rules booklet so they're aware of the specifics on what is available or how to use appliances in your place, provide the WiFi password again (if you provide Internet as part of your

booking), tell them that you are always available and if they have any concerns, they should contact you so you can resolve it immediately.

4. **During their stay:** It's good practice to drop your guest a message to touch base, ask them if they're enjoying their stay and if they have what they need with a gentle reminder that you're available should they need to contact you at any time. If you provide any house-keeping service during the stay, make sure you mention this as well and what the process is for cleaning or restocking to be carried out. This reassures your guest that you are available at all times and attentive to their needs. If you have a guest book, encourage your guests to write in it. Make sure you have a request for review or star-ratings either near or inside the guest book to maximize the chances of getting reviews and star-ratings.

5. **Day before check-out time:** Your guest might be getting a bit stressed about the trip back home, so whatever you do, please don't add to their increasing stress levels. Keep this message concise, remind them of the process for checking-out, and if there's anything they need to do ahead of checking out.

6. **Post departure:** Drop your guest a "thank you for staying at our place, it was an absolute pleasure to host you" type of message. This is the time to ask for a review from your guest, whilst it's fresh in their minds and mention that you will do a review for them as well, if that's what you plan on doing. If you plan on giving your guest an excellent review, don't be shy to tell them that when you drop them a message. You never know, by the laws of reciprocity or karma, you may get some good reviews and star-ratings for your good deed. By making this part of your process, you remind guests that reviews and ratings are important, and hopefully you get those good reviews and ratings coming.

These key moments can turn an average guest experience into a great experience that your guests will remember for years to come.

If you plan on hosting many guests, you will notice that some of these message types can become repetitive as you provide nearly identical details or answer similar questions over and over again. In addition, the timing of these messages can be spaced out according to the duration of the booking. For example, the welcome message, WiFi password, or thank-you-for-staying messages won't drastically change from guest to guest and these messages can be issued to guests at certain points in the timeline.

Utilize scheduling, templates, and any software or applications that platforms like Airbnb offer to make your life as a host significantly easier. Be sure to modify the templates to use wording that you're happy with and update the schedules for any automated messages to be sent to guests.

Here are a few tips to take into account when it comes to communicating with guests:

- Spell-check your messages and templates

- Find a balance between communicating when necessary and over communicating (which might annoy or overwhelm your guests)

- Keep all communication on the platform so that there is documentation in case of disputes later on

Do not underestimate the importance of good communication between you and your guests. Get it right, and your guests will feel like they were treated like royalty–which increases the chances of getting great reviews and star-ratings. Get it wrong, and all parties will feel frustrated that they're not being heard, or worse, their needs are not being met–I don't need to spell out what this will do to your reviews but it won't be a pretty sight. Pick which side of the fence you want to be on.

Maintenance on Speed Dial

We had just arrived at our hotel after a long flight, and of course, the toilet did not flush properly. Fortunately, we were moved–upgraded–to another room, and all was fine after that unpleasant incident.

Imagine a guest arrives at your place, and their first experience is that of a broken toilet; hardly the best first impression you want to make. These things will happen, but it's how you handle it that determines whether you'll be successful with STRs.

Plugged toilets are one of the many problems you may face when running an STR. Any appliance, piece of furniture, flooring, or decoration is subject to being touched or used in some manner. This is simply the nature of the beast when it comes to the STR business. More guests equal more potential profits but also more wear and tear in general.

I touched on some of this earlier under the property management section, but let's dig deeper into the preparation you need to do *before* something needs fixing or replacing. Regardless of whether you self-manage or hire a property manager or company to deal with any of the maintenance work, prepare yourself to handle any maintenance issues that may crop up at a moment's notice. You don't need to stock up on every appliance, flooring, paint, wiring, or nuts and bolts that's used in your STR to be prepared for something breaking down. You do, however, need to have the means to replace or fix things if and when something breaks down during a guest's stay.

First off, you need cash or money readily available to pay contractors at a moment's notice. Have a budget that can accommodate labor and material costs of the usual suspects, such as bath or shower, toilet, appliances, and any other items or area that you believe are most prone to breaking down. Typically, this would be the high-usage areas and appliances that have the highest probability of breaking down first. Personally, I would allocate a budget for this and *not* dip into the emergency fund, which is there for real emergencies and not maintenance issues.

Next, make sure you're able to have things fixed or replaced as soon as humanly possible. Your guests are paying you good money, so your place has to live up to their expectations and broken appliances and the like simply won't cut it. If you're using property management services, they need to be on the ball and have contractors on the job within hours, not days, and definitely not weeks. If you're hiring contractors, have them on speed dial ready to fix the problems you or your guests might have. Naturally, if you're doing all the maintenance yourself, be ready to adjust your normal schedule of work or commitments to accommodate maintenance issues that can and will come up when you least expect it.

With any of these approaches, it's wise to have a few contractors on speed dial, so if one or two are unavailable, you can lean on the ones that can assist you. In fact, have someone who can assist you to manage these contractors like a trusted friend, neighbor, or family member–this is for those really tough times when you're unavailable, but your guests need something urgently fixed. You might be under quarantine in a foreign land and unable to get home to remedy a broken oven that you would normally fix yourself and it's at these times that you can leverage those backup plans we discuss here.

You may want to incorporate an inspection after every guest or on a regular basis (something like once a week or once a month) to make sure everything in your STR continues to function as it should. Any maintenance issues you spot during these inspections can be remedied before it gets more serious, and guests start complaining about it.

More Than Cleaning

Let's make this clear: you will never be remotely successful in the STR business if you do not have a strong system for cleaning, or housekeeping. Don't let anyone tell you otherwise. Of course, you need to be great at the other aspects of this business, but if you present a filthy, unkept and poorly presented space to any guest, they will obliterate your listing with complaints to the platform along with reviews that would rate in the negative numbers if such a thing were possible. Not to mention, you will also see a rise in refund requests where you not only lose the booking, you lose the income too—rightly so, no one pays top dollar to live in a pigsty.

The aim is to get your place cleaned up and re-staged to five-star (or better) hotel standard. These standards need to be replicated every time a guest leaves, ready for the next guest. *Every. Single. Time.* There are three ways to accomplish the clean and re-stage process. You can: a) hire a cleaning company to do all of the cleaning, b) hire and train people to clean according to your specific needs, or c) do all of this yourself. Whichever approach you take, make sure the finished product is clean, well-presented, and that this process can be consistently replicated for every guest.

Don't let this innocent word cleaning fool you. There's a lot more to it than washing floors, wiping windows, or dusting off areas. The demands placed on cleaners extends beyond a simple clean but includes other actions such as restocking, laundry service, informing you of any damages, taking pictures or videos of the condition your STR is in (both before and after a guest stay if possible but especially if there's damage), re-staging your STR as it is advertised on platforms, and more. We'll refer to cleaning as the whole bundle and the cleaning crew you hire, regardless of whether this is a cleaning company, individual cleaner, or yourself if you plan on doing this work, as your cleaning crew.

You and the crew need to be *on the same page*. For example, if you expect your crew to clean surfaces, replenish consumables like coffee pods or candy, document with video or photos any damages from the previous guest, and re-stage your space for the next guest, then make sure your crew understands all of this and can deliver on it. If you're in doubt, create a checklist on every single action that you want your crew to take for each room or area and run through this with them so that there is no ambiguity and expectations are clear.

Before you get your cleaning processes planned out, consult the *platform's guidelines* for cleaning policies as well as local and national law requirements. There may also be additional guidelines introduced as a result of some unexpected event such as the coronavirus pandemic of 2020, that you may need to adhere to. These rules may change every so often and it's a good idea to revisit these rules regularly to keep yourself up to date.

Once you know what the policies and guidelines are, it's time to get a cleaning process in place for every area and room in your STR. Let's take the bathroom space as an example and list out a very detailed process:

- Initial inspection of bathroom to assess how previous guest left the bathroom–if possible, document with pictures and videos (time and date stamps included) to be taken before cleaning, especially if there is any evidence of damage

- Clean and sanitize toilet, bathtub and/or shower, sink, and faucet

- Remove any hairs from sink, bathtub or shower, and floor

- Remove dirty bathroom linen and replace with clean linen

- Remove garbage from bin and replace with fresh bin lining

- Replenish toilet paper and facial tissues

- Replenish complimentary toiletries (if you provide this)

- Dust and disinfect all areas, especially high-touch areas, such as door handles, light switches, toilet handle, and vanity surface

- Mop or vacuum (depends on the type of flooring you have) bathroom flooring

- Clean tiling and grout surfaces

- Clean and disinfect mirrors

- Stage bathroom as presented on platform listing

- Final inspection of bathroom–if possible, document with pictures and videos (time and date stamps included) post-cleaning for next guest

- Collect dirty bathroom linen (along with linen from the rest of your space) to be laundered

You don't need to get this detailed with your cleaning process as long as the clean is done properly. Professional cleaners will typically have a grasp of all of this so won't need any training, but you may need to train other cleaners to the standards you require.

Your crew need to not only clean the place, but document pre and post-clean, and put things back where they were initially positioned as well. Remember earlier, we talked about staging your place and getting fantastic pictures? If you stage your place in a complicated fashion (thousand-piece puzzle style), this makes it more difficult for the crew to put things back the way they were.

Coordination and scheduling need to become second nature to you. When a guest checks out, you need to get the crew in before the next guest checks in. You'll need to be on the ball with this as any slippage here will likely have a negative impact down the line. If your crew takes three hours (on average) to turn your place around, then make sure you factor in the checking in and out of guests with a buffer since some guests may request an earlier check in or a later check out.

The worst thing to happen is your place is not ready for the next guest due to a clash in scheduling or the clean and maintenance take longer than expected. Whilst most guests will leave your place largely in the same state that they found it in, some might leave more of a mess or damage appliances, and this will need to be made good before the next guest arrives. If your STR has great demand, you may be tempted to have back-to-back bookings with minimal time for cleaning and maintenance in order to maximize income and profits. My suggestion is to give yourself some breathing room between check-in and check-out times so that your clean and maintenance crew can remedy any problems. Don't have check-out time at 1pm and a check-in time of 2pm, this is unlikely to be enough time for any crew to turn things around and leaves you with no breathing room in case things go wrong. A typical check-out time might be 10am or 11am with a check-in time around 3pm or 4pm. This would give you four to five hours for your crew to work their magic between guests. In the event that you allow a guest a later check-out time, make sure there's enough time for the cleaning crew to work their magic before the next guest checks in.

> **Tip:** have a backup plan in case your usual crew can't clean your STR between guests. The regular crew might be unavailable due to sickness, holidays, or unforeseen circumstances. If you have a few other services on speed dial, you reduce your chances of getting stuck.

7 Ways to Fail – Don't Do These

No one likes failing, but you know what people dislike even more? Losing money, especially if they could prevent it.

So far, we've talked about things to get right in order to maximize your chances of being successful but are there things you need to avoid? You bet there are.

In the unfortunate event that you find yourself identifying with some of these, learn from your experience and move forward with a positive attitude.

1. Micromanagement and snooping. No one likes being spied on and micro-managing your guests' behaviour can be detrimental to guests enjoying their stay.

Micromanagement is especially true for house-share type arrangements where you're sharing some areas with your guests such as the living room, refrigerator, kitchen, or dining areas. Some things might irk you. For example, maybe the guest didn't wash their cup after a sip of their coffee, and you might be inclined to tell them to wash up immediately.

An example of snooping might be that you notice the lights in their room are left on late at night or overnight and you inform the guest that they need to turn the lights off after a certain time. Unless there is a local law against keeping the lights on in your bedroom late at night or overnight, you might be overstepping and making guests feel uncomfortable knowing that you're watching their every move. Is this how you'd like to be treated if you paid good money for a place and had the host checking up on what you're doing, even if it's completely within your rights as a guest?

Put yourself in your guests' shoes and ask how you would feel if you experienced these actions? You'll likely receive feedback from guests, directly or indirectly. One way that guests share their feedback is through reviews which will reflect how they felt about their stay. They may share their views with you privately and if they do, thank them for their honesty and learn from this experience.

2. Guests' requests. A bit of discretion is required when it comes to guests' requests but don't dismiss any request out of hand just because it's inconvenient for you to arrange. We're not talking about outrageous requests like getting a full refund after a guest has had a great stay. No one is expecting an Olympic-sized swimming pool with valets lined up to provide you with complimentary towels or slippers, especially if it's not detailed on your listing.

Think more along the lines of housekeeping or convenience that some guests might expect from either staying at hotels or places similar to yours. Some of these convenient items might be:

- Additional blankets and bathroom linen

- Having a portable heater should guests need extra heat in a room or area

- Toiletries such as complimentary toothbrush, toothpaste, soap, or shampoo

These aren't unusual items for hosts to offer guests or for guests to request. If one guest requests it, it's entirely possible that future guests might request for it too. You can, of course, flat out say you will not provide anything that guests request–you are, after all, the host.

Saying that, if it's within your power and doesn't cost too much in terms of budget or time, it's probably worth the investment and guests might appreciate these items. This will make their stay more enjoyable which can lead to repeat bookings and good reviews.

3. Losing your temper is not a good look and seldom has the desired effect on guest experience. There will be many times where your patience is tested during your real estate journey. This can range from irritating guests, poor support from the platforms you're listing with, or scheduling clashes to name just a few potential problems.

I encourage you to zoom out and take every experience, good or bad, as a learning experience. All experiences are feedback for you which should be received with a calm and cool head. If you lose your composure, you risk upsetting guests or people you're dealing with and this in turn does not usually make them want to deal with you more.

When was the last time you got yelled at by someone and then felt you wanted to do more for that person? I certainly can't remember a time like that in my life, ever.

4. House rules should be concise, to the point, easy to understand, and even easier to implement. I've seen house rules as long as tax laws and somehow guests are expected to not only read all of it, but comply with every detail.

If you were greeted by a fifty-page book of house rules, how inclined are you to read it from front to back? On the off chance that you do read the whole thing, will you remember every rule that you need to adhere to? I'm going to guess that it's possible that you read the whole fifty-page book of house rules but you're highly unlikely to remember all of it, much less observe any or all of the rules.

Keep your house rules simple and easy for guests to both understand and comply with.

5. Leaving too much on the table. I'm not suggesting you put a whole lot of effort into milking a few cents here and there on your nightly rate. The effort-to-profit ratio simply would not be worthwhile. However, missing out on a lot of profit because you're not tuned in to important and popular local events will probably leave you weeping inside.

It's your place, you need to know what goes on in the local region. If there's a big concert, a sports event, or any event that will attract a crowd, then you need to know when, where, and how to adjust your pricing accordingly.

If you're unsure of how to price your listing around these events, you can check out other listings in the area for around the dates of an event and see the going rate. Some events take place annually and you'll have a feel of pricing once you've hosted around the time of that event once.

Fair warning here. Some guests are very well-organized and book many months ahead in anticipation of these popular events. You do not want to be under pricing your place simply because you're unaware of an event that will take place in your location.

Stay up to date with what's going on in your region. There's no need to be the most expensive listing against your competition, but you certainly don't want to be missing out on too much profit as a result of your ignorance of these popular events.

6. You might be the weakest link. It's a given that you should have backup service providers in the event that your preferred resource is unavailable. We've touched on this in relation to cleaning services or maintenance contractors but having backup plans extends far beyond these two factors.

Have you planned for the possibility that, for whatever reason, you may be unavailable when a guest is about to arrive for their stay? Perhaps you've been held up in another country and the flight got cancelled due to bad weather and there's no internet or phone services for the critical hours that your guest is attempting to reach you. Maybe you went in for what you thought was a routine minor surgery that took a lot longer after which the hospital puts you in an induced coma to monitor your progress, thus making you unavailable to the world. Wouldn't you know it, these are always the times that guests might need you.

With this in mind, is there someone who can run things for you in case you're unavailable for a few hours or days? Not many people want to think about worst-case scenarios where they are incapable of attending to their business, but you have to plan for this just in case it happens. Your STR business needs to continue and booked guests must be attended to, regardless of your situation.

Make sure whomever you choose to step in for you on short notice is capable of handling your business in the short term and can deal with things like guest queries, the cleaning crew, contractors, to name a few things. You may want to have a meeting with whomever you pick to explain what is required of them along with all the main contacts and processes so that they can step in at a moment's notice. They need to know how your business runs and be able to "run with it" as it were.

7. Some you win, some you learn. Let's face it, no journey is ever without its pain and suffering. Although most guests are awesome, you will no doubt go through some pretty dreadful experiences on your STR journey. The option to exit this business is always available at any time–but it would be a shame not to learn from these unfortunate experiences and capitalize on it for the future.

With every bad experience, you must make it a point to learn from it. For example, a guest takes advantage of your good nature and brings in pets even though you have a strict no-pet policy. The pets proceed to defecate, claw, and chew around what seems like every inch of your place. Or maybe your guests have a big fight and damage your property. This would be a terrible experience for any host to go through. You'll face varying degrees of guests violating your rules or space at some point in time.

Here are a few options available to you when faced with horrible guest experiences:

- Throw your hands up in the air, put the property up for sale, sell at a deep discount because it's in such a state of disrepair

- Refurbish your entire property to an equal or higher standard than before, charge additional fees and obtain increased insurance coverage to cover damages to your property

- Possibly install external cameras to monitor for unwelcome additional guests or pets (make sure you declare cameras on your listing according to platform rules)

- Greet the guests on arrival to confirm they have no pets

If damage to your STR happens, refer to the platform's rules and any insurance they may have in place for damages. The point is that you have many options available to you and exiting the business is merely one of them.

If you learn from these experiences, you will be savvier when it comes to guest bookings in the future and dealing with similar issues won't scare you at all because you know how to deal with the fall out.

If you learn from every guest experience, both good and bad, and through the sharing of experiences with others in your STR-related network, you'll be ahead of those who don't learn, much less think about improving.

Chapter 11: The Talk

This isn't a "birds and the bees," or where-do-babies-come-from, talk. Thank goodness! But it isn't far off.

When you're at the start of your STR journey, the first payout from hosting that first guest is a precious memory. It's also proof that you *can* do this. For many, that first payout serves as a major confidence booster. This is especially true if you've been swimming against the tide of popular belief from your inner-most circle of friends and family, none of whom have any experience with real estate investing, voicing their opinions about how you won't be able to make a success of this.

With this initial success under your belt, you may be thinking about expanding your real estate investing empire. A noble cause indeed! However, before you do that, and without taking anything away from your initial success, we need to have *the talk*. You know, the one about whether scaling up is truly what you want or if there are other ways to achieve your goals.

Some people get fixated on the idea of achieving financial freedom or some financial goal through *only* real estate investing, closing their minds off to any alternatives. There's nothing wrong with achieving financial goals with only one investment vehicle, real estate in this case. However, it would be negligent of me if I did not tell you that you can look beyond real estate.

Many investors are happy with one or a handful of real estate investments, whilst others might dive deeper and get multiple properties or deploy other real estate investing strategies. It's easy to get carried away and think that real estate investing is the only game out there–it isn't. Truth is, you can make money in just about anything if you know how. Ask a successful stock market trader and they'll tell you that trading the stock market is the best thing since sliced bread–it might be for them, but this may not work for you. Similarly, ask someone who is successful in a certain business or investment arena, and the answer they'll give you is that their method is best, because that's what worked for them. Again, what has worked for them may not work for you.

The question you need to ask yourself is this: do you want to maintain, reduce, or expand with STRs or real estate investing in general? There are no right or wrong answers here. I've mentioned this before, but life happens. For example, at this point in your life, real estate investing might be awesome for you where you're at the top of your game, juggling your full-time job (which you love) with your real estate investments whilst you're a singleton. A few years down the line, you might meet that someone special and decide you no longer have the energy, will, or interest to keep up with your real estate investments and may choose a different real estate investment strategy or exit the real estate investment universe in favor of other alternatives.

Don't fall into the trap of thinking you have to stick with real estate investing from now until the end of time. Do what makes sense for you. If this means more real estate in your portfolio, fantastic. If you want to explore and diversify into other investment vehicles, don't let anyone stop you.

Now that you know you're not bound to real estate investing for all eternity, let's take a look at diversification. We will look within the real estate universe or through different asset classes, followed by a discussion about scaling up if you decide you want more of that awesome sauce called real estate investing.

Chapter 12:
Diversification

Y ou may find it odd to find a chapter NOT talking STRs in an STR book, but believe me, you need to read this. We can't have a discussion about scaling up until we've had a serious conversation about diversification. Stay with me here. You'll see what I mean shortly.

Let's start off by addressing the elephant in the room. Why do you need to diversify? I want to answer this question by walking you through the typical journey of someone buying their first investment property. For starters, let's observe that the vast majority of us don't start off investing in multiple properties or units when we first dip our toes into real estate. Most of us, myself included, start off with one property and apply one real estate strategy, such as the STR or long-term rental approach. Running one property can be quite a risky proposition. A change in any of the following can have a significant impact on your investment property:

- Property area affected by change in law

- Impact of local or global economy

- Change in tenant or guest demand

- External factors such as weather, war, global pandemic, or other major factors

A combination of one or more of these problems may, or may not, come to pass, but it does demonstrate how vulnerable having only one investment property can leave you. If you are relying on the income from this one investment property and have no other income streams, then you better hope you experience none of these for a period beyond what your emergency funds can handle. On the opposite end might be an investor called Dave. Dave has multiple investment properties scattered across the country or internationally, caters to different tenant or guest-types, and deploys different real estate investment strategies. Dave is diversified across different strategies and locations and is therefore more able to weather any problems that a single property may cause.

You can diversify by investing in the real estate space or in other asset classes. Here are some ideas on how you can diversify your income streams with STRs or beyond:

- Invest in STRs in different locations and/or targeting different guest-types

- Invest in other real estate strategies such as long-term rentals, commercial, flips, and more

- Invest in other, non-real estate related, businesses

- Invest in companies or a group of companies across different industries, sectors, countries, or regions through the stock market

Evaluate the returns you anticipate achieving and understand the true cost of any investment you plan to take on. Some will take more effort on your part but will produce a higher return whilst others may provide a lower return but are relatively more passive.

As you conduct your research into other potential income streams, be aware that there is always an *opportunity cost* of pursuing one approach over another. For example, if you invest your capital in another STR that can produce a ten-percent annual return, that means you're not able to invest in other ventures (using the same capital) that provides potentially, say a fifteen-percent annual return. This is the opportunity cost of choosing the STR investment over another investment.

In addition to the opportunity cost, consider as well how an investment might perform over many years and what the *compounded return*, where the profits are reinvested periodically, might be. There are no guarantees of what the future holds, which is why there is a standard disclaimer in most investment brochures that says something along the lines of past performance is no guarantee of future performance. Rightly so as no one can predict the future. However, for research purposes, it's a good idea to see what the compounded returns have historically been so you can take this into account as a guide, not an expectation.

> ***Caution***: when searching for information, especially on how best to invest your capital, beware of confirmation bias[10]. The best defense against confirmation bias is to seek out information that goes against what you're seeking–yes, it's an odd thing, but let me explain why you need to do this. When you search for anything along the lines of *"how to get rich using [insert the subject you're looking into],"* search engines like Google will typically show you the most relevant search results. These search engines are unlikely to show you results such as *"[insert the subject you're looking into] is a scam and you will lose all your money"* because that's not what your searched. Seek a balanced view or gather information so that you can form a balanced view. Weigh up the pros and cons before forming an opinion on whether to look deeper into any potential investment vehicle.

Personally, the main investment vehicles I use are real estate and the stock market. These offer me a satisfactory balance between the returns and true cost according to my risk tolerance. In my years of research, I've found that there's no holy grail of investment that offers guaranteed exponential returns whilst being one hundred percent passive and hands-off. It simply does not exist. Saying that, I'm very happy to be proven wrong on this, so if you come across any investment vehicle that you believe is the holy grail of investment vehicles (one that offers astronomical as well as guaranteed returns that is also fully passive), please drop me a line–if it pans out, I might even buy you a beverage of your choice!

No matter how you choose to diversify, do your research thoroughly and consult qualified professionals and people who have travelled down the route you want to take and heed their words of wisdom.

Chapter 13: Key Ingredients to Scaling Up

Having tasted success with one STR, your thoughts turn to the future and all its possibilities. You may be full of hope and, in your mind, will be floating some of the common questions, such as:

- How would having more than one investment property change my life and that of my loved ones?

- Am I willing to get more invested in real estate?

- Can I really achieve financial freedom and retire early?

- Is it really possible for me to leave my job to pursue my passion and hobbies?

After all, you've got one successful investment property under your belt. It's merely a simple matter of rinse-and-repeat the process, right?

As you ponder the possibilities of expanding your real estate portfolio, I want to anchor you back down to Earth a little–just a little–to keep you grounded. Can you achieve all your financial goals, retire early, and reach the so-called lean or fat F.I.R.E. (financial independence, retire early) through real estate investing? Yes, I believe you *can* achieve all this and there are lots of examples out there of people who have successfully accomplished this using real estate as the sole investment vehicle. You merely need to do a quick search on the Internet or find real estate focused YouTube channels or podcasts and you'll come across lots of these examples.

However, there are no guarantees with any investment strategy, and you may not achieve the same level of success that others have obtained, or portray to have obtained on social media. Be cautious of what you see on the Internet and social media when it comes to success stories since there's no way for you to verify the results, how they got the results, or what they went through to achieve them. You need to run your own race and focus on what works for you. Also, comparing your results to others is not a productive use of your time and is akin to keeping up with the Joneses. As the modern day saying goes, your mileage may vary (ymmv) when it comes to the level of success you can achieve[11]. For example, a seasoned real estate investor will likely have more equity or capital to invest than a new investor, who is working hard in their day job, with limited income and doing all they can to save every penny they can for a down payment. It will be much easier for the seasoned investor, armed with more capital as well as experience and contacts, to buy more properties compared to the new investor.

With your feet firmly planted on the ground, let's get down to business. There are three main ingredients that are required for investors to make a great success in the real estate space. Here are the three ingredients:

- Financing

- Real estate deals

- Systemize the process

With these three ingredients, you'll be able to grow your real estate portfolio to the levels that you desire. For some, this will be a few investment properties, let's say anything between one and five. For others, this might be five or more properties. That's it. It's that simple, only three ingredients required! Yes, I said it, simple.

Do not confuse simple with *easy*. Some investors make buying more real estate look easy, but there's often a backstory to the ease at which they get financing, find, and manage great investment properties. For example, deals may appear to come easy to some investors but when you dig a little deeper, they have spent countless hours building up relationships with realtors or building contractors who know exactly what investment properties they're looking for–from run down properties that need a big development project to properties that only require a basic touch up to bring it to market standards; building relationships with your network takes time and effort and doesn't happen overnight but can be very rewarding.

You may be in a *hurry* to scale up, but slow and steady wins the race. Even with the best of financing, deals, and a great system, scaling up isn't an endeavour to be taken lightly and definitely not something you want to rush. If anything, you should scale up only when you have healthy emergency funds to weather major storms to your investments and any leverage that is deployed is firmly under control. One of the biggest risks is over-leveraging and when things don't go well, you might end up going bankrupt.

Warren Buffett said it best: *"No matter how great the talent or efforts, some things just take time. You can't produce a baby in one month by getting nine women pregnant."*

This statement applies perfectly to rushing the process of scaling up your real estate investment portfolio. Try as you may, some things take time; the right deal has to come along, the right financing needs to be in place to take advantage of the deal, and the timing of any or all of these factors can't be forced.

Financing the Empire

We covered some of the basics earlier on in the section *Two Main Ways to Financing* but that was focused on getting one STR investment property. The two main methods remain the same; you can use cash or leverage a mortgage with banks. However, when it comes to scaling up, there are additional nuances that you'll want to know earlier rather than later so you can plan in advance accordingly. Let's take a look at each of these methods as applied to scaling up safely and effectively.

> **Note:** it's possible to craft unique arrangements to finance your empire using the so-called creative financial approach. If you plan on doing this, make sure you're crafting win-win deals for all parties and consult legal professionals for support. These transactions are private business arrangements between two or more parties, and you are therefore free to negotiate and agree (or disagree) to

any terms and conditions that all parties put forward. The more seasoned investor takes this approach and it isn't an approach that investors who are new to real estate investing should look at until they have more experience. The vast majority of investors I've met initially scale up using cash or leverage mortgages through banks before looking at unique arrangements (if at all) and this is what we'll focus on.

Scale with cash. To buy more real estate with cash, you need to save up as much of the profits you have from your current portfolio of investment properties. This is in addition to other sources of income you may have. Depending on the price of real estate, this may be a tough one to accomplish, but it's possible and gets easier the more investment properties you have.

For example, one investment property might generate, say, ten thousand dollars of net profit a year. If you're looking to invest in a property that is worth fifty-thousand dollars, then you'll need to save up for five years before you're able to purchase that next investment property–assuming you're recycling the profits from your first investment property only. With two properties (of the same kind), you'll generate twenty-thousand dollars in profit a year, which will only require you to save up for two-and-a-half years to buy the third property, and so on.

You can speed up this process by saving up as much as you can from your investment properties and any other sources of income you may have, much like how you saved up for that first investment property. This process is typically slow at the start of your journey, but once you have a few investment properties, you'll be able to generate cash at a much faster rate and scale up faster and faster. This is where the snowball effect takes place; it takes time to build momentum but once you get it going, it's unstoppable when rolling down a snowy mountain.

Scale with mortgages. This is where you need to lean on good mortgage brokers (qualified and experienced with real estate investor needs and lingo) that have access to a wide range of lenders. In addition to this, your broker must be familiar with, amongst other aspects, arranging financing for larger real estate portfolios beyond the basic first-time buyer client, terms and conditions of the main lenders, processes of the main lenders, and the time it might take to arrange for a mortgage or remortgage (the term remortgage may also be referred to as refinance).

Typically, you'll need to have some kind of down payment on a property and take a mortgage out on the remainder of the value of the property. For example, if you want to buy a property of two hundred thousand dollars, you may need to put a down payment of twenty-five percent or fifty-thousand dollars, and borrow the remainder of seventy-five percent or one hundred fifty thousand dollars from a lender, such as a bank. You'll need to come up with the down payment for every property you purchase, and this might come in the form of saving up cash from your job, investments, business, remortgaging to release equity on a property or properties that you already own, recycling capital from a fixer-upper style real estate strategy, or by other means. Once you've got the down payment side covered, you need to truly understand lenders.

All lenders will have limitations which they will express in their terms and conditions. These limitations reflect their risk tolerance, business practices, as well as the rules and regulations in your country. Typically, lenders can place limitations on a wide range of factors, such as, but not limited to, some of the following:

- Type of investment property or real estate strategy they're willing to lend on

- Maximum amount they're prepared to lend an individual or a company (depending on how you structure your investments)

- How they calculate the amounts they're prepared to lend and what they base these calculations on

- Whether they consider your entire real estate portfolio as part of their lending criteria (this is sometimes referred to as portfolio lending)

- Minimum time between remortgaging a property

You'll need to work closely with your mortgage broker to understand lenders' policies, processes, and time it so that you can finance more real estate investments as and when they come up.

Here's an example of why understanding each lender's terms and conditions is important. Let's take a look at one potential condition–minimum time between remortgaging a property. You buy a property that needs some fixing up and plan to remortgage at the end of the refurbishment project. You finance this investment by taking out a mortgage with lender A with a view to remortgaging with the same lender as soon as possible in order to recycle as much of the original capital into the next project. The idea is that after the works is completed, the value of the property will have increased sufficiently in order for you to remortgage at the same loan-to-value and extract the original capital (or more) that you had put in as a down payment. In the terms and conditions, lender A has a minimum of twelve months from the time you purchase the property before they will allow for a remortgage and closing the mortgage early carries a hefty fee. In your mind, you think this is not going to be an issue as it'll probably take about one year to refurbish this property anyway, since the property is in great disrepair. On the refurbishment project, weather and luck favors you and the work is completed within three months. Sadly, on the remortgaging side of things, you're now stuck, unable to remortgage earlier due to the early-closing fees which equates to the entire refurbishment cost, too high a price to pay and one which you're unwilling to stomach. As a result, you will have to endure nine months with lender A before you can seek other options. With hindsight, it would have been preferable to choose a lender with flexible-to-no mortgage exit terms that allows for an earlier remortgage. How quickly you can remortgage a refurbishment project can play a critical role in how fast you can move on to the next project, and therefore scale up.

Another example might be where you want to get a mortgage with a specific lender that offers great mortgage interest rates and excellent terms and conditions, but you're unable to use this lender because your real estate portfolio size is beyond what they would consider based on their maximum portfolio size limits. This lender might have a limitation on the maximum personal portfolio size of one million dollars, but your portfolio is currently valued at three million–they are definitely not prepared to offer any mortgages to you based on your portfolio size exceeding their criteria. You could have utilized this lender earlier on in your journey to take advantage of their offering.

There are a lot of moving parts when scaling with mortgages. Your best bet is to get an outstanding mortgage broker to discuss your plans and what you'll need to put in place, understand the main lenders' terms and conditions, how these lenders operate, and strategize in advance so that you know which lenders are available to you at different points in your real estate journey.

In my experience, mortgage brokers that focus on first-time, or one-time, buyers will not understand the needs of an investor who intends to have multiple properties and hence multiple mortgages. This is not to say these brokers can't learn or do the job for an investor who is looking at multiple properties in the long term, but it does mean potential missed opportunities and maybe delays as both you and the broker have to take time to understand each lenders' terms, conditions, processes, and so on. One-time buyers are not concerned with portfolio maximums, time between refinancing, or how different lenders apply different criteria to arrive at how much you can borrow on a mortgage–these are questions that more experienced investors are concerned about, and you will fall in this category if you plan on scaling up your real estate portfolio. It's in your best interest to get a broker who speaks the scaling up real estate portfolio lingo to make your life as easy as possible.

Real Estate Deals

In order to add more properties to your real estate portfolio, you first need to find them. The two main ways to finding deals are:

- On your own

- Leverage your network.

Either way, this doesn't mean once you find a property, you can simply buy it without any due diligence. Due diligence is a must, regardless of whether or not a deal looks good on the surface.

Finding real estate deals **on your own** will be more time consuming than if you leverage your network. There's twenty-four hours in a day and only so much one person can do. It's quite literally impossible to be everywhere, doing everything, at the same time. This means that you will eventually be limited to how much time you can allocate to finding more investment properties to add to your portfolio, at which point, it will make sense to leverage your network.

When you're looking at potential real estate deals, you know exactly what you want. As you evaluate factors such as WWHRO, local STR or rental rules and regulations, you can determine if a property is likely to fulfil your criteria or not. Before diving deep into the due diligence process, you'll want to see that a potential property at least ticks off some of the main points that are your line in the sand. For example, you may have some of the following as a minimum criteria:

- Type of real estate: apartment or house

- Located in a high-demand STR urban locations

- Within a budget of five hundred thousand dollars

- Ready-to-market on platforms like Airbnb (minimal to no work required)

- Generates a potential minimum of three percent gross yield per month

In this example, if you find a property that ticks off most of these points, then you are happy to dig deeper and conduct further due diligence. On the other hand, if the majority of these points are not satisfied, you may choose to move on and continue your search rather than force this property to fit within your criteria or adjust your criteria to fit the property.

At some point, it will make sense to **leverage your network** in order to get deals coming your way. This isn't like making instant coffee where you scoop out coffee powder and simply add hot water; you can't call a random realtor, sit back, relax, and expect that the best of the best real estate deals to fall into your lap. Networking takes time and is based on relationship-building with people who are predominantly within the real estate industry. It's possible to get deals from people who are not usually in the real estate universe such as neighbours, friends, family, and acquaintances but chances of this happening are relatively low. Typically, people who are most likely to bring up deals are people who have their eyes on the market constantly–realtors, salespeople, deal hunters or people who find deals for a commission, and fellow investors.

Before reaching out to your network, you'll want to nail down the main criteria that you absolutely must have in any property. These are your non-negotiables or red line of minimum criteria that need to be met. If one of the criteria is that a property must be ready-to-market with minimal or no work required, you need to communicate this to your network. Other criteria may be the budget you're working with or the type of property or location that you want. Set your own minimum requirements and be prepared to negotiate on other terms and conditions. Using our coffee analogy this is akin to being willing to negotiate on how much milk, cream, or sugar you add to your coffee, but not negotiating on the brand of coffee you'll drink or type of cup in which the coffee must be served.

It will take a bit of time to form relationships and train your network for your needs. That's the bad news. The good news is, once your network is aware of what your tastes are, they may throw deals your way when they come across them. There will be some stumbling blocks, but the clearer you are with what you're looking for, the higher the chances of your network bringing the kind of property deals you're looking for to you.

> **Tip:** Don't be the novice. The novice, and I speak from experience as I was once a novice, will go out, look to buy the next property they set their eyes on, and see things through rose-tinted glasses—with a mountain of confirmation bias. Back in the day, my enthusiasm to get the next property was so powerful that it overcame logic and common sense. Knowing full well that a deal wasn't great, I would adjust my criteria (cash flow and other requirements) to lower targets, use overly optimistic figures in calculations such as potential rent or income, assume pessimistic cost figures because I'm awesome at controlling costs or getting great bargains, and have an incredibly difficult time being objective as to whether a deal was truly a good deal or not. This was partly because I was passionate, but also because my motivation was to achieve financial independence as soon as humanly possible. Sadly, that's not how things work in the real world. Good deals don't pop up every minute of every day, just waiting for you to add to your portfolio. Plant your feet firmly on the ground, assess things objectively as if you were investing your seventy-year-old grandmother's whole life-savings, and ask yourself: would I really put my grandmother's life savings on this deal? Assuming you love your grandmother dearly and are not a scumbag that is happy to gamble away a loved one's life savings, you'll assess deals with more clarity.

Systems to Make Life Easier

When you go through the process of adding more and more cash flowing properties to your real estate portfolio, there's a high chance that you will repeat some, if not most, actions you carry out and it's worth mapping out the process for numerous reasons, some of which we alluded to earlier on. As a brief recap, here are a few of those reasons:

- Clarity of where each party fits in and when their expertise is required for continuity of operations in case something happens to you

- Never overlook important matters

- Identify problems or areas of improvement early on

The alternative would be to not have any processes in place–this is perfectly fine, especially if you're only adding one or two properties to your portfolio or go many years between deals. However, if you plan on growing your portfolio with multiple deals over the course of, say, one to five years then you will repeat many of these actions. It will be to your benefit to set up and follow a process that you're happy with in order to take advantage of some of the points mentioned.

For any rental investment property, there are three main categories for which processes can be mapped out:

- Buying processes

- Operational processes (running a property)

- Selling processes

Identify the areas that have repeated actions and map out the process that you go through. For example, the buying process may look something like this:

1. Confirm financing is in place and estimated budget before beginning search for property.

2. Find a property that fits the criteria of a good real estate deal.

3. Estimate potential rental income and vacancy rates.

4. Estimate all costs to get property ready for rental market (from fixing up, staging, to professional photos, costs to operate as a rental unit, and more).

5. Perform cash flow calculations with estimated figures (use your own custom template if you have one).

6. If cash flow calculations are satisfactory, perform further due diligence to operate said property as a rental unit such as license requirements, legal obligations, and so on.

7. Double and triple check the cash flow calculations and due diligence information.

8. Consult with legal and accounting teams to confirm any aspect of due diligence and calculations are correct and there are no additional rules or regulations you need to factor in.

9. Make an offer and negotiate to get as good a deal as possible.

10. If offer is accepted, transaction to go through all the usual subsequent stages (realtor, lawyer, mortgage broker, bank, and so on) – you can expand on this further.

This is a high-level view of what one part of the process might look like to add a property to your real estate portfolio.

Once you add a property to your portfolio, the next stage is to follow your process of getting the property ready for the rental market. Again, you can create a whole bunch of processes or checklists to ensure that all aspects are covered and nothing major is overlooked. For example, even if the property doesn't need any fixing up, you may need to hire an interior designer, furnish, and stage the property along with getting professional photos done before marketing the property. Once the property starts getting guest bookings, you can map out the process such as dealing with guests or tenants from onboarding to departure or complaints, and more.

There may come a time when you decide to sell some, or all, of the real estate in your portfolio. Whether this is part of your exit strategy, or you simply want to cash in after a great run, if there are repeatable actions, then feel free to put processes in place. Unless you're selling your entire real estate portfolio to one buyer, it's likely that you'll need to furnish buyers with some information for each property, such as taxes, any updates made to the property along with the details, and so on.

How in depth you choose to get into when mapping out your processes is completely up to you. My suggestion is to at least cover the major factors that are non-negotiable to you and allow leeway for more minor aspects. For example, it would be unacceptable for me to proceed with buying a property if I had not consulted with my lawyer for legal support. As such, it would be part of my process that when buying a property, checking in with my lawyer is a must. Some people may not want, or need, legal support–perhaps they're happy to buy in an auction and the terms and conditions are set out by the auction company.

Going one step further, you can create checklists to ensure that you don't miss anything that is detailed in your processes–be sure to only check off something after you actually do it.

What's Your Next Stop?

S o, will you get into the short-term rentals market? There is no right or wrong answer.

Although there are no guarantees in life, significant rewards await those who are willing to take the risk and invest in real estate. It won't be a walk in the park if you get into short-term rentals. Do your best to make it work, but if it doesn't work out, know that there are other avenues you can explore.

There will be difficult as well as happy times. Squeeze every last drop of learning opportunities from both negative and positive experiences, as this will help you grow for the future.

One thing I hope that we can agree on is that there are no shortcuts. Due diligence, tedious and boring as it may be, cannot be overlooked or brushed aside–unless you're in a hurry to lose all your money.

Whatever you choose to do, know that I am in your corner and wish nothing but the best for you in the future–real estate investing and beyond.

Raising a glass to your future successes,

Andy

Acknowledgements

Life throws all sorts of challenges in our direction and it's up to us to find the silver lining amidst the gloomy clouds. The global pandemic, for all its problems and hardships, allowed me the time to write this book. So, in a funny way, I'm grateful for the opportunities that the global pandemic of 2020 brought us.

The writing and publishing community has been an awesome and supportive community where I've learned so much. The writing sprints have been especially productive. I'd like to extend special thanks to Jacob Rothenberg, Dale L. Roberts, Zee Irwin, Nick Nawroth, and Michael Murray for generously sharing their knowledge and experience.

I would be completely and utterly lost without Mandy and my parents. Thank you for all the love, support, and encouragement, especially in my darkest hours. I love you.

Finally, I want to thank you, the reader, for taking time out of your life to read this book. I hope you find what works for you.

About the Author

Andy Wen is an author and investor, investing in both real estate and the stock market. Andy believes in crafting wealth from diverse sources and never being dependent on one source of income. He aims to keep investing super simple and preaches straightforward but effective investment strategies.

In his free time, Andy enjoys playing the piano, spending time with his wife, and teaching his cat, Twinkle, tricks that might make them both famous one day.

Don't forget to follow Andy at:

- **YouTube** – MoneyTalksWithAndy.com/YouTube

- **Facebook** – MoneyTalksWithAndy.com/Facebook

- **Website** – MoneyTalksWithAndy.com

Resources

Recommended websites:

https://www.airbnb.com

https://www.airdna.co

https://www.biggerpockets.com

https://www.booking.com

https://www.furnishedfinder.com

https://www.google.com/maps

https://www.investor.gov/financial-tools-calculators/calculators/compound-interest-calculator

https://www.investopedia.com

https://www.mrmoneymustache.com

https://www.openrent.co.uk

https://www.realtor.ca

https://www.redfin.com

https://www.rightmove.co.uk

https://www.thesaurus.com

https://tradingeconomics.com

https://www.vrbo.com

https://www.zillow.com

https://www.zoopla.co.uk

Book recommendations:

More Than Cashflow – Julie Broad

The Simple Path to Wealth – J.L. Collins

Property Investment for Beginners – Rob Dix

The Millionaire Real Estate Investor – Gary Keller

Rich Dad, Poor Dad – Robert Kiyosaki

The Bogleheads' Guide to Investing – Mel Lindauer, Taylor Larimore, Michael LeBoeuf

Cash Uncomplicated – Aaron Nannini

I Will Teach You to Be Rich – Ramit Sethi

Quit Like a Millionaire – Kristy Shen, Bryce Leung

The Millionaire Next Door – Thomas J. Stanley, William D. Danko

The Book on Rental Property Investing – Brandon Turner

Never Split the Difference – Chris Voss, Tahl Raz

Notes

Chapter 1

1 Miller, Zoë, "15 foods that are called different things around the world," Insider, accessed February 3, 2022, https://www.insider.com/foods-different-names-ar ound-the-world-2018-10#brits-say-crisps-americans-say-potato-chips-2.

Chapter 2

2 Aydin, Rebecca, "How 3 guys turned renting air mattresses in their apartment into a $31 billion company, Airbnb," Insider, accessed February 3, 2022, https://www.businessinsider.com/how-airbnb-was-founded-a-visual-history-2016-2.

3 Kenton, Will, "Comparables," Investopedia, accessed June 15, 2022, https://www.investopedia.com/terms/c/comparables.asp.

4 Flint, Jessica, "The Vacation Rental Business Is Coming of Age," The Wall Street Journal, accessed December 11, 2021, https://www.wsj.com/articles/the -vacation-rental-business-is-coming-of-age-11629392453.

Chapter 3

5 Maverick, J.B., "What Is the Average Annual Return for the S&P 500?" Investopedia, accessed February 11, 2022, https://www.investopedia.com/ask/an swers/042415/what-average-annual-return-sp-500.asp.

6 Interest Rate, Trading Economics, accessed November 25, 2021, https://trad ingeconomics.com/country-list/interest-rate

Chapter 4

7 "A Restaurant Business and Technomic Special Report," Restaurant Business, accessed December 13, 2021, https://www.restaurantbusinessonline.com/top -500-chains.

Chapter 6

8 Avatar (2009 film), Wikipedia, accessed January, 5, 2022, https://en.wikipedi a.org/wiki/Avatar_(2009_film).

9 "Data is our business. Accuracy is our mission." AirDNA, accessed March 27, 2022, https://www.airdna.co/airdna-accuracy.

Chapter 12

10 Scott, Gordon, "Confirmation Bias," Investopedia, accessed July 5, 2022, https://www.investopedia.com/terms/c/confirmation-bias.asp.

Chapter 13

11 "YMMV," Cambridge Dictionary, accessed July 8, 2022, /https://dictionary .cambridge.org/dictionary/english/ymmv.